LEARNING FOR LIFE AND WORK 2

NI Key Stage 3

P. Dornan, K. Armstrong,
L. Curragh, J. McCusker,
J. McCurdy and L. McEvoy

The Publishers would like to thank the following for permission to reproduce copyright material:

Photo credits

p.3 *TL* © Isitsharp/Fotolia; *TR* © Elena Elisseeva/Fotolia; *CL* © Caroline Schiff/Getty Images; *CR* © Jana Lumley/Fotolia; **p.5** © Corbis; **p.6** *TR* GreenGate Publishing; *CL* © Inti St Clair/Getty Images; **p.7** © Jeff J Mitchell/Reuters/Corbis; **p.8** *TL* © Sachs500/Fotolia; *TR* © Denis Anikin/Fotolia; **p.11** GreenGate Publishing; **p.12** *CB* © Bettmann/Corbis; *BL* © E.O. Hoppé/Corbis; **p.13** *TR* © Bettmann/Corbis; *CB* © Mike Kemp/Getty Images; **p.19** © Loungepark/Getty Images; **p.25** © Marvin Koner/Corbis; **p.26** © NatUlrich/Fotolia; **p.27** *TL* © Jip Fens/Fotolia; *C1L* © Christopher Dodge/Fotolia; *C1* GreenGate Publishing; *C1R* © Jan Prchal/Fotolia; *C2L* © Chad McDermott/Fotolia; *C2* © PhotoCreate/Fotolia; *C2R* © Kimberly Reinick/Fotolia; *BL* © Lisa Accardi/Fotolia; *CB* © Andrew Brookes/Corbis; *BR* © Haruyoshi Yamaguchi/Corbis; **p.29** *T* © Saniphoto/Fotolia; *M* © Nicholas Homrich/Fotolia; *B* © Andres Rodriguez/Fotolia; **p.32** © John Kelly/Getty Images; **p.33** © Bettmann/Corbis; **p.40** Courtesy of Equality Commision for Northern Ireland; **p.43** Posters courtesy of Equality Authority and The Equality Commision for Northern Ireland; **p.44** Company logos courtesy of Chinese Welfare, Disability Action, Age Concern and Gingerbread; **p.47** *TR* © John Bailey/Fotolia; *C* © Michael Chamberlin/Fotolia; *BR* © Absolut/Fotolia; **p.48** © Peter Turnley/Corbis; **p.53** Logos courtesy of Save the Children, Make Poverty History, ActionAid, Age Concern, Trocaire, CAFOD, Christian Aid, WaterAid, Oxfam and Habitat for Humanity; **p.54** © Tom Stoddart Archive/Getty Images; **p.55** ATD Fourth World; **p.56** *TL* © Forgiss/Fotolia; *BL* © Poco_bw/Fotolia; *TR* © Victorpr/Fotolia *BR* © Andres Rodriguez/Fotolia; **p.57** © Tomasz Trojanowski/Fotolia; **p.58** Logos courtesy of The Simon Community Northern Ireland, Save the Children, Northern Ireland Anti-Poverty Network and Barnado's Northern Ireland; **p.60** *TL* © Ammer, CartoonArts International/CWS; *BL* © Yayo, CartoonArts International/CWS; *TR* © Schrank, CartoonArts International/CWS; *BR* © Medi, CartoonArts International/CWS; **p.64** Courtesy of the Jane Tomlinson Appeal; **p.65** © FAO/P. Ekpei; **p.66** *L* © Tom Morrison/Getty Images; *CL* © Carlos Davila/Alamy; *CR* © Steve Skjold/Alamy; *R* © Jim West/Alamy; *B* © Kevin Cooley/Getty Images; **p.67** © Laurent nicolaon/Fotolia; **p.69** *T1* © Bettmann/Corbis; *T2* © Gideon Mendel/Corbis; *L* © Pressmaster/Fotolia; *CL* © Hulton-Deutsch Collection/Corbis; *CR* © Construction Photography/Corbis; *R* © Hulton-Deutsch Collection/Corbis; *B1L* © Andres Rodriguez/Fotolia; *B1R* © Jaroslaw Grudzinski/Fotolia; *B2L* © Pawel Libera/Corbis; *B2R* © Edsweb/Fotolia; **p.70** *L* © Allstar Picture Library/Alamy; *R* © David Leven 2006; **p.71** © David Lefranc/Kipa/Corbis; **p.73** *TL* © Guy Massardier/Fotolia; *BL* © George Disario/Corbis; *CT* © Rosie Greenway/Getty Images; *CB* © Stephen Coburn/Fotolia; *R* © Klikk/Fotolia; **p.74** Courtesy of Christine Boyle/Lawell Asphalt; **p.75** Courtesy of Muck 'n' Muffins; **p.76** *TL* © Stephen Coburn/Fotolia; *BL* © Leah-Anne Thompson/Fotolia; *C* © Kevin Penhallow/Fotolia; *TR* © Roman Milert /Fotolia; *BR* © Stephen Coburn/Fotolia; **p.77** *T* © ZM Photography/Fotolia; *B* © Poco_bw/Fotolia; **p.78** *TL* © Monregard/Fotolia; *BL* © Sasha/Fotolia; *C* Courtesy of RFD Beaufort; **p.79** *TC* © Helene Rogers/Alamy; *TR* Araraadt/Fotolia; *BR* © Spuno/Fotolia; *C* Courtesy of RFD Beaufort; **p.81** Courtesy of Biffa; **p.84** *L* © Dennis Tokarzewski/Fotolia; *C* © Sonya Etchison/Fotolia; *R* © Gideon Mendel/Corbis; **p.86** © Randy Faris/Corbis

Acknowledgements

p.30 Buckley Publications for the article from *Business Eye Magazine*; **p.32** *The Independent* for the article 'Girls allowed: FA lifts its ban' by Mary Woolf; **p.35** *The Belfast Telegraph* for the article 'Female migrant workers experience widespread mistreatment'; **p.64** Jane's Appeal for the text on Jane Tomlinson; **p.65** FAO for the article from FOA Newsroom; **p.70** *The Guardian* for the article 'I don't want praise' by Vicki Frost; **p.78** RFD Beaufort

Every effort has been made to trace all copyright holders, but if any have been inadvertently overlooked the Publishers will be pleased to make the necessary arrangements at the first opportunity.

Although every effort has been made to ensure that website addresses are correct at time of going to press, Hodder Murray cannot be held responsible for the content of any website mentioned in this book. It is sometimes possible to find a relocated web page by typing in the address of the home page for a website in the URL window of your browser.

Hodder Headline's policy is to use papers that are natural, renewable and recyclable products and made from wood grown in sustainable forests. The logging and manufacturing processes are expected to conform to the environmental regulations of the country of origin.

Orders: please contact Bookpoint Ltd, 130 Milton Park, Abingdon, Oxon OX14 4SB. Telephone: (44) 01235 827720. Fax: (44) 01235 400454. Lines are open 9.00–5.00, Monday to Saturday, with a 24-hour message answering service. Visit our website at www.hoddereducation.co.uk

© Peter Dornan, Kathryn Armstrong, Lois Curragh, John McCusker, Jim McCurdy, Lesley McEvoy 2008

First published in 2008 by
Hodder Education,
part of Hachette UK,
338 Euston Road
London NW1 3BH

Impression number   5 4 3 2
Year   2013 2012 2011 2010 2009 2008

All rights reserved. Apart from any use permitted under UK copyright law, no part of this publication may be reproduced or transmitted in any form or by any means, electronic or mechanical, including photocopying and recording, or held within any information storage and retrieval system, without permission in writing from the publisher or under licence from the Copyright Licensing Agency Limited. Further details of such licences (for reprographic reproduction) may be obtained from the Copyright Licensing Agency Limited, Saffron House, 6–10 Kirby Street, London EC1N 8TS.

Cover photos: *main image* The Mourne Wall and Mourne Mountains © Alain Le Garsmeur/Corbis; *top images* royalty free.
Illustrations by GreenGate Publishing Services, Alex Machin and Barry Glennard
Typeset in 11/14 pt New Century Schoolbook and ITC Franklin Gothic Book by GreenGate Publishing Services, Tonbridge, Kent
Printed in Italy

A catalogue record for this title is available from the British Library

ISBN: 978 0340 927 090

CONTENTS

Introduction — 1

Personal Development

1. What is my true self? — 2
2. What is the basis for self-confidence? — 4
3. How can I think more positively? — 6
4. What is 'being responsible' anyway? — 8
5. Can I wait for what I want? — 10
6. How do I fire my imagination? — 12
7. Is the risk worth taking? — 14
8. How can I handle emotions safely? — 16
9. How do I learn to trust? — 18
10. How can I become assertive? — 20
11. How do I decide what is right or wrong? — 22
12. How can I learn from mistakes? — 24
13. Why do we use drugs? — 26
14. What is addiction? — 30

Local and Global Citizenship

15. What is equality? — 32
16. What causes discrimination? — 34
17. What are the different types of discrimination? — 36
18. How does the law protect people from discrimination? — 38
19. What is the role of the Equality Commission? — 40
20. How can we promote equality? — 42
21. How do NGOs promote equality? — 44
22. What is social justice? — 46
23. What is poverty? — 48
24. What are governments doing about global poverty? — 50

25	What can I do about global poverty?	52
26	Is poverty a human rights issue?	54
27	Is there poverty in Northern Ireland?	56
28	How can we tackle poverty in Northern Ireland?	58
29	What have I learned about citizenship?	60

Education for Employability

30	How have I changed?	62
31	What are enterprising people like?	64
32	How can I be enterprising?	66
33	Why do employers want enterprising staff?	68
34	What is an entrepreneur?	70
35	Could I be an entrepreneur?	72
36	Who are the entrepreneurs in our local businesses?	74
37	Why are small to medium employers so important?	76
38	How do businesses support each other?	78
39	How can businesses make themselves green?	80
40	How do businesses make sure they are safe places to work?	82
41	How can I learn to be a responsible employee?	84
42	Why is teamwork so important in the workplace?	86
43	What type of job will I do?	88

Answers 90
Index 91

INTRODUCTION

Hello and welcome! *Learning for Life and Work*'s aim is to help you to achieve your potential and to make informed and responsible decisions throughout your life journey of growth and change. The purpose is to help you develop:

1 as an individual (mostly but not only through Personal Development),
2 as a contributor to society (mostly through Local and Global Citizenship),
3 as a contributor to the economy and environment (mostly through Education for Employability).

Each book in the course is divided into these three main sections and then broken down into topics. Each topic has a big question as its title to investigate. Throughout the topics you will find the following features.

Learning intentions

Each topic starts by outlining the learning intentions – these are the skills and knowledge you should be learning as you make your way through the topic.

Activities

Each topic has a number of activities. You may be asked to work as an individual, in pairs, in small groups or as a class. The activities have a structure, but because each person and group is unique, there is room for you to be unpredictable and come up with something that no one else has thought of. The activities work best when you are enthusiastic, give them a go and develop and agree some helpful ground rules for working with others. Have fun!

Thinking skills and personal capabilities

Alongside each activity there is an icon. There are five different icons in all and these signpost the main thinking skills and personal capabilities you will be developing while carrying out the activity. The following table shows which skills each icon stands for.

Skill	Icon	Description
Managing Information		Research and manage information effectively to investigate personal development, citizenship and employability issues.
Thinking, Problem Solving, Decision Making		Show deeper understanding by thinking critically and flexibly, solving problems and making informed decisions.
Being Creative		Demonstrate creativity and initiative when developing ideas and following them through.
Working with Others		Work effectively with others.
Self-Management		Demonstrate self-management by working systematically, persisting with tasks, evaluating and improving own performance.

Personal journal

Some activities are designed to encourage you to keep a personal journal. This will help you understand three key questions:

1 Where have I been?
2 Where am I now?
3 Where do I want to go?

Personal journals will help you make sense of your journey and are a particularly useful tool to help assessment. This means your personal journal may be seen by your teacher, family or classmates. It may be personal but it won't be private!

1 WHAT IS MY TRUE SELF?

Learning intentions

I am learning:
- ✓ to understand what the difference is between my ideal and real self
- ✓ to accept myself, both the good and the bad.

In life, we are all becoming, developing and changing for better or for worse. There is always a gap between who we are (our *real self*) and who we would like to be (our *ideal self*). This gap creates a tension inside us. The skill is to allow this tension to be helpful, healthy and productive so that it pushes us to develop into a better person.

Who I am now (Real Self) ←— This gap creates a tension. —→ **Who I'd like to be (Ideal Self)**

The tension is helped by our desires, hopes and dreams and ways we develop to cope with life.

 ## Activity 1 A self-assessment

a) When you think about the 'way it should be' in your life, what do you desire, imagine or dream of? Contrast this with the way things really are in your life at present. Use this information to copy and complete the table below.

Area of my life	The ideal (my dream)	Reality at present
My looks		
My family		
My friends		
My finances/pocket money		
My school work		
My clothes		
My house		
My boyfriend/girlfriend		
My school		
My personality		
My skills		
My attitudes		

How we deal with this tension either creates hope, a future and a motivation to change and develop, or it can lead to hopelessness, despair and being stuck in life.

b) What does the tension between these two columns make you think and feel?

Let's look at how four different people deal with the tension in their lives between the real and the ideal.

 Arthur doesn't value or take notice of anything that is less than ideal. He denies anything that is weak or bad in his life. As a result he needs to pretend and deceive himself and others about his real self. His life is an act, and occasionally Arthur realises he is a hypocrite; however, facing reality is too difficult, so he keeps pretending. He believes it is better to look right than to be right.

 Michelle doesn't believe that there is anything good in her life, or that anything good will happen in her future. As a result she won't make plans for the future or accept any compliments. She cares about very little. She just keeps her head down and gets on with what comes her way.

 Amy can only accept what is good. When she sees anything less than good, it is unacceptable, so she attacks, judges and criticises it. She complains and criticises others regularly and she constantly drives herself to be perfect. She knows she can only be acceptable to herself and others if she is perfect.

 Frank neither denies the ideal nor the bad. He accepts and forgives the weak or less than perfect in himself, while still holding on to the ideal as a possible goal that he plans and works hard for. He is both happy with himself and yet making plans and taking action to change for the better.

Activity 2 — How do I deal with the tension?

Most of us are a combination of the four people above. We either

- Deny the bad/weak/less than ideal.
- Deny the good, while discouraging hope and a future.
- Judge and criticise.
- Accept, forgive, be kind and move forward.

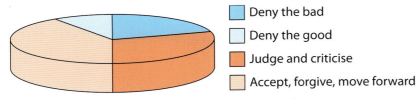

a) If you were to divide the four areas into percentages, what percentage would you give each response in your life so they all added up to 100 per cent?
b) Which response do you use most regularly in your life?

In groups of four:
c) Discuss what life would be like for each of the four people above.
d) Work out a strategy for each that would help them develop into a person who could deal better with the tension between the ideal and the real.

 Activity 3 — Personal journal

'I am happy with myself but I am not yet all that I can be.'

a) Reflect on what you need to do so that this statement could reflect your life.
b) Using the diagram below, where are you on the journey to self-acceptance?
c) In light of this, how would you like to personally develop?

2. WHAT IS THE BASIS FOR SELF-CONFIDENCE?

> **Learning intentions**
> *I am learning:*
> ✓ to understand the nature of self-confidence
> ✓ how self-confident I am in different situations.

Understanding confidence

Confidence is the trust or faith we have that a person or a thing can do what we expect them to do. Self-confidence is having faith in yourself and what you can do. If we have self-confidence, it is like oil that lubricates what we do in life and makes it go smoothly. Every day, as we face different situations and activities, we find ourselves either self-confident, unconfident or over-confident.

People with high self-confidence typically:

- have little fear of the unknown
- are able to stand up for what they believe in
- have the courage to risk embarrassment
  (for instance, by giving a presentation to a large group of people).

Activity 1 How self-confident are you?

Look at the situations below. Estimate how confident you would be in each circumstance and answer the following questions:

a) Would you be quietly self-confident, over-confident or lacking in confidence?
b) Why would you feel this way?
c) How would you act in each situation?

Situations

1. Standing up on your own in assembly to give a 'thought for the day' in front of the whole school.
2. Walking into a room full of strangers at a party.
3. Asking somebody out who you feel is 'out of your league'.
4. Taking a different point of view from the rest of your group of friends and everyone knows it.
5. Being first to discover a person who is unconscious and bleeding on the street after a hit-and-run car accident.
6. You are chosen as a representative of your school to meet the First Minister and Deputy First Minister of Northern Ireland, to talk to them about your school and community.

The three broad states of confidence could be described as:

Unconfident	Self-confident	Over-confident
An unconfident person gets paralysed and can't function due to worry. They have lots of self-doubts and become very critical about themselves. This causes a vicious cycle where the worry cripples the person into inaction, and they continue to beat themselves up, creating more anxiety and worry, so that they perform even more ineffectively.	When the anxiety is just right, you are at your best. You know that negative outcomes are possible, but rather than exaggerating them or playing them down, you give them the attention they need (what can I do if this happens?). You are as prepared as possible, with the courage to have a go.	In the absence of anxiety a person could become careless due to over-confidence. An over-confident person doesn't see the need to consider all the possible outcomes, and is sure the outcome will be what they want and expect. However, pride often comes before a fall!

 ## Activity 2 Role-plays around confidence

a) In groups of four, choose four of the situations from Activity 1. Act out each situation three times. (Rotate the four roles with each scenario.)

1 Group member one: in an over-confident way.
2 Group member two: in an unconfident way.
3 Group member three: in a self-confident way.
4 Group member four: act as an observer making notes of the differences between the different levels of confidence.

Below are some suggestions to consider when you are acting, and what the observer could look out for:

- Body posture
- Eye contact
- Voice (loudness, pitch and tone)
- Passion and belief
- How real, genuine or fake did they appear?
- What actions or behaviour did they show?
- How prepared did they appear?
- How did they cope with the unexpected?

b) In your groups, make a list of characteristics and a list of actions for confident people, as you work out:

- who confident people are, and
- what confident people do.

c) On the basis of your list, do you consider yourselves to be confident people?

 ## Activity 3
Personal journal

a) Take some time to note down the situations where you are:

- over-confident
- under-confident
- self-confident.

b) What have you learned through this topic that would help you prepare for life in a more confident way?

Confident student giving a presentation

3 HOW CAN I THINK MORE POSITIVELY?

Learning intentions

I am learning:
- ✓ to understand the health benefits of positive thinking
- ✓ to identify my negative thoughts and turn them into positive ones.

Is your glass half empty or half full? How you answer this age-old question may reflect your outlook on life and whether you're optimistic (a positive thinker) or pessimistic (a negative thinker).

In fact, studies show that these personality qualities, optimism and pessimism, can affect how *well* you live and even how *long* you live.

Be positive: Live longer, live healthier

All people talk to themselves through thoughts. We call those thoughts *self-talk*. We do it so often, we don't always notice it. It's like a radio playing in the background, unnoticed but there all the same. If the thoughts that run through your head are mostly negative, your outlook on life is pessimistic. If your thoughts are mostly positive, you're probably an optimist.

Researchers continue to explore the effects of optimism on health. The health benefits of positive thinking include:

- Decreased stress
- Greater resistance to catching the common cold
- A sense of well-being and improved health
- Reduced risk of heart disease
- Breathing more easily if you have breathing problems
- Improved coping ability for people with cancer
- Living longer
- Better coping skills.

Positive thinking is good for your health

Activity 1
Internet research

a) Type in 'health benefits of positive thinking' into any internet search engine like Google, and see if you can find any research or evidence to support or deny that positive thinking makes a person more whole or healthy. Remember to use all the parts of a whole person.

b) Do you think it is worthwhile for you to think positively? Explain.

Put a positive spin on negative thoughts

Think of your mind as a garden. In any garden there is usually a mixture of weeds and flowers. Let's say that the flowers represent positive thoughts and the weeds are negative thoughts. Your job, as the gardener of your mind, is to encourage and develop the flowers and to remove any weeds that choke and spoil your life, health and well-being.

Turning negative self-talk into positive self-talk will improve your outlook. If you tend to have a negative outlook, don't expect to become an optimist overnight. But eventually your self-talk will automatically contain less self-criticism and more self-acceptance.

The weeding process seems simple, but it takes time and practice to turn positive thinking into a regular habit.

Activity 2 Practice makes perfect

Here are some examples of typical negative self-talk in the left-hand column. In groups of four, see if you can come up with a positive twist on each of the phrases. Two have been filled in as examples, but you may have better ideas. Try to be as original, creative and positive as possible.

Negative self-talk	Positive spin
I've never done it before	
It's too complicated	
I don't have the resources	
There's not enough time	
There's no way it will work	
I don't have the ability	
It's good enough	There's always room for improvement
It's too much to change	
No one bothers to talk to me	
I'm not going to get any better at this	
I'm not good enough	
I can't do it	I'll have a go. I can't do it yet

Activity 3 Encouraging one another

Many professional athletes get top sports training and coaching in positive thinking to help them achieve their goals – and it works! The same can apply for us. A 'can do' attitude may be just what it takes to start a healthier lifestyle. Get into a group of four with a chair in the middle:

a) Each person should take turns in the 'hot seat' and think of one thing in their life about which they regularly say 'I can't do it'.
b) This person should share this with the group, and then the rest of the group should make suggestions about how to think positively about it.
c) The person should say which suggestions they find helpful, and which they don't, and why.

Activity 4 Personal journal

Over the next 24 hours carry a notepad around with you. Use it to jot down your self-talk. Stop at various times and write the thoughts that you are thinking, particularly the ones that you repeat regularly. If these are negative thoughts, look closely at them and see if they are real, helpful, or based on reason. See if you can turn them into positive thoughts that are optimistic.

4 WHAT IS 'BEING RESPONSIBLE' ANYWAY?

Learning intentions

I am learning:
- what being personally responsible means
- to accept personal responsibility in my life
- to examine my options and consider the outcomes of taking personal responsibility.

When you were born, you were not responsible for anything. You were totally reliant on your parents for everything you needed.

Now that you are growing up you have to take more and more responsibility for a whole variety of things, for example what you wear, cutting the grass, getting your bag ready for school, doing your homework.

Activity 1 When do I become responsible?

Individually:

a) Look at the list of activities below and jot down at what age you think someone should become responsible for each.

- Choosing what to wear
- Feeding yourself
- Getting up in the morning
- Doing your homework on time
- Passing exams
- Buying your own clothes
- Organising a holiday
- How happy you feel

In groups:

b) Compare your answers.

- Has everyone chosen the same ages?
- What factors influenced your decisions?
- Was there anything on the list that you felt was not your responsibility yet? Why?

You cannot be responsible for everything that happens to you, but you can be responsible for how you think and feel and act when something happens.

This is not as easy as it sounds! We all blame others for what has happened to us, from time to time, or blame ourselves for something that we cannot be responsible for.

Activity 2 What am I responsible for?

In pairs look at the situations below and agree what you would and would not be responsible for. Give reasons. Consider the advantages and disadvantages of taking personal responsibility.

- You are upset because the barbeque you had organised for a large group of friends was spoiled by the rain.

- You get a school detention for messing about in science class.

- You arrive home from school to find your mum is really upset because a close friend has died.

- You spend so much time chatting on the internet that you don't get your homework finished. You decide to copy from a friend and get caught. The teacher punishes you and your friend, and now your friend isn't speaking to you.

- Your best friend blames you for the break-up of a relationship because you wouldn't agree to provide an alibi to his/her parents and she/he wasn't able to meet up with his/her boy/girlfriend.

- You are going out for the evening and you find the top you want to wear unwashed on the floor under your bed.

 ## Activity 3 Personal journal

a) Identify one area in your life where you need to accept personal responsibility. Activity 1 may help to provide you with some ideas.
b) Create some steps for how you plan to go about this.

5 CAN I WAIT FOR WHAT I WANT?

> **Learning intentions**
>
> *I am learning:*
> - to understand what delayed gratification means
> - to develop the muscles in my will, to achieve better self-control, and to learn to wait for what I want.

In the last topic we looked at how to manage ourselves and our lives better by taking personal responsibility. Another skill in self-management is delayed gratification. This is the ability to wait, often with discipline and hard work, in order to get something that you want. This is sometimes called patience. People who lack this often need things immediately and may suffer from poor self-control. Our bodies constantly shout at us (impulses), so our decision-making part (our will) needs strong 'muscles' so that we have the ability to control ourselves and not give in to every urge.

Activity 1 My experience of waiting

Get into pairs and share any experience you have had of having to wait for what you want. Was it good, bad or indifferent?

Activity 2 Applying the skill of delayed gratification

Here are the sorts of characteristics associated with people who can't wait and need immediate or instant gratification (left-hand column) compared with those who can wait and delay gratification (right-hand column).

Instant gratification	Delayed gratification
1 I'll have it NOW!	I'm prepared to wait for it until later.
2 I exert little or no effort.	I exert a little to a lot of effort.
3 I avoid pain for a short-term gain, but have no long-term benefit.	I endure short-term pain for a long-term gain.
4 My body impulses control me and I give in to them.	I control my body impulses and decide whether I give in to them or not.
5 I live for the present.	I enjoy the present but live with the future in mind.
6 I take the waiting out of wanting.	I develop patience and self-discipline through waiting and working for what I want.
7 I do whatever feels good.	I choose to do what is best.
8 I avoid pain at all costs.	I face pain, and work through it when I have to.
9 I am easily tempted.	I am able to say yes and no if necessary.
10 Life happens and it is done to me.	Life happens and I set goals, choose carefully, and respond thoughtfully.
11 I have poor boundaries.	I have well defined boundaries in my life.
12 I will give up quickly and rarely finish anything, especially when it's hard work.	I will stay the course and finish things as well as I can.
13 I will blame everyone else and avoid taking personal responsibility.	I will take personal responsibility for my life.

The following table applies these opposite attitudes to real-life choices. Get into pairs, and discuss which you think is best in each case, delayed or instant gratification:

Instant gratification	Delayed gratification
Drinking alcohol under-age	Waiting until 18 to drink
Spending my money now!	Saving money for something I really want
Eating any snack now!	Waiting until dinner time
Being lazy	Carrying out a programme of regular exercise
Experimenting now in a sexual relationship	Keeping sexual activity for a committed relationship
Studying all night before an exam till you're exhausted	Making a programme for exam revision

For each of these activities:

a) Outline the pros and cons of instant versus delayed gratification.
b) Do you think it is worth waiting or not? Explain.
c) Think into the future and guess what life would be like for a 40-year-old who had delayed gratification around these activities as a teenager, compared with somebody who had lived for the moment. Which would you rather be?

Activity 3 Developing the muscle of your will

How strong is your will and ability to control your impulses? Can you delay getting what you want? In order to find out we need to do a longer-term experiment. You are going to stop eating something you enjoy until the next class. Why not try chocolate (or something else if you don't eat chocolate). Look out for impulses to eat chocolate, recording when and why you get these feelings.

- Were you able to stop eating chocolate until the next class? How long did you last?
- What impulses did you feel, once you realised you couldn't eat it?
- How easy or difficult did you find it to not give in to your impulses?
- How good are you at delaying gratification?
- What do you think this means for your future? (Apply this to debt, alcohol, relationships or something else.)

6 HOW DO I FIRE MY IMAGINATION?

Learning intentions

I am learning:
- ✓ to work out what imagination is
- ✓ to see with my mind's eye
- ✓ to use my imagination to create hopes and dreams for my future.

Activity 1
Exploring imagination

In pairs:
a) Discuss what you think imagination is. Write out a definition.
b) We talk about seeing with 'the mind's eye'. What does this mean, and what can you see with it? (If you have difficulty, close your eyes and just say what you see.)
c) Does your imagination have limits?

Throughout human history, many leaders have pointed to the importance of hopes and dreams as an essential part of life. A few examples are quoted through this topic. In Topic 1 we looked at the gap between who we are and who we would like to be, and the methods we develop to cope with the difference. In this topic we want to explore how we need to use our imagination to develop hopes and dreams which motivate us and create desire for growth and change. When the going gets tough, hopes and dreams give us strength inside to help us to keep going and not give up. They act like a compass to point us in the right direction.

Imagination is our ability to represent or picture things to ourselves in our minds. We can imagine things possible and impossible, good or bad, positive or negative (see Topic 3). We have all had the experience of worrying about something and imagining terrible things that never happened.

At a basic level, to plan ahead and personally develop involves imagination – the ability to think about something which does not yet exist (the new us!). More than that, what we are able to imagine will shape what we believe and choose to do in life.

Nothing happens unless first we dream.

Carl Sagan (1934–1996, astronomer and astrobiologist)

You see things; and you say, 'Why?' But I dream things that never were; and I say, 'Why not?'

George Bernard Shaw (1856–1950, Irish playwright, critic and political activist)

 **Activity 2** Using our imaginations to help Sarah

In groups of four:

a) Read the information about Sarah below.

Sarah is a 13-year-old girl who was born in inner-city Belfast. She lives with her mother, two older brothers and two younger sisters. Her father left her life when she was eight years old, and she hasn't seen him since. He was an alcoholic and sometimes was physically violent. Her family are very poor and life is often a struggle to make ends meet. When Sarah looks in the mirror, she is not sure if she is pretty or lovable. Although quite clever, she is not sure what to do about the future, as people around her don't often go to college or university. She can't decide whether it is a good idea to try for a career or not. Sarah is really artistic, excelling at art, rhythm and dance. She attends a local youth club, and has been involved in local dance competitions. In a Personal Development class, she is asked to consider what she thinks her life will be like when she is 40 years old, and to use her imagination to create four hopes and dreams.

b) Now create a diagram like the one below to show how you could help Sarah. Along the four main spokes of different colours, write four hopes and dreams that would create a positive future for her. (They could be concerning career, family, relationships, activities and interests, education, achievements, etc.)

c) Against the three branches coming out of each of the spokes, write three things that Sarah would have to do or develop in her life in order for those dreams to become reality.

Imagination will often carry us to worlds that never were. But without it we go nowhere.

Carl Sandburg (1878–1967, American poet and historian)

Activity 3 Personal journal

a) How active and helpful is your imagination?

b) Draw a diagram about yourself like Sarah's. Create four hopes and dreams, and three things that you would need to do in order to make each of those dreams become reality.

Personal Development

13

7 IS THE RISK WORTH TAKING?

Learning intentions
I am learning:
- to identify risks in the things I do in life
- the skill of managing risk.

Life is full of choices and consequences. Almost all the choices we make have some degree of risk. A risk is when we hope for a good outcome, but at the same time we expose ourselves to the possibility of harm, loss or danger.

So are risks worth taking? Life with too much risk is full of stress and often short! However, life with no risk is dull and boring. We are often looking for some sort of risk and thrill to help us rise above the ordinary. The big challenge is how to measure risk so that it is calculated to give us the best outcomes with as little possible chance of harm.

Activity 1 — Sharing risks

In groups of four:

a) Share past experiences in your lives and come up with the five most risky things that you have done as individuals, with the most risky at the top of the list.

b) Each group in the class shares their top risky activity and the whole class comes to an agreement about the top five most risky events.

Introducing The 'I AM' risk management process

If we want to get better at taking and avoiding risk, we need to find a process to help us make good decisions. We are going to use the 'I AM' risk management process. I AM can help you remember the three key steps in this process:

- **Identify** the risk
- **Assess** the level of risk
- **Manage** the risk.

Each of these three parts has different elements to complete, outlined in the diagram below.

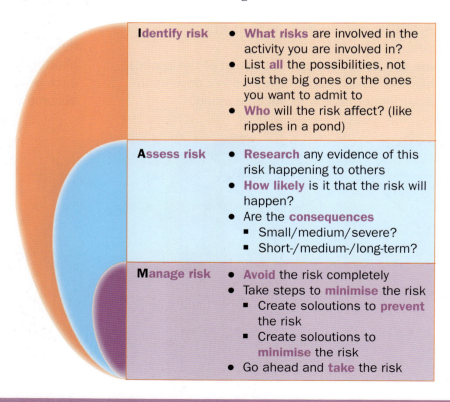

Identify risk
- **What risks** are involved in the activity you are involved in?
- List **all** the possibilities, not just the big ones or the ones you want to admit to
- **Who** will the risk affect? (like ripples in a pond)

Assess risk
- **Research** any evidence of this risk happening to others
- **How likely** is it that the risk will happen?
- Are the **consequences**
  - Small/medium/severe?
  - Short-/medium-/long-term?

Manage risk
- **Avoid** the risk completely
- Take steps to **minimise** the risk
  - Create soloutions to **prevent** the risk
  - Create soloutions to **minimise** the risk
- Go ahead and **take** the risk

Activity 2 — Learning that 'I AM' a risk manager

In groups of four, apply the process shown in the diagram on page 14 to the situations listed below.

a) Identify the risk or risks involved and who they might affect.
b) Assess the probability, level and length of risk involved.
c) Manage the risk by deciding which of these three responses you would make:

- avoid it
- minimise the risk (tell us how)
- take the risk.

The scenarios are:

1. Jumping from an aeroplane 6000 m in the air to raise money for a local cancer charity.
2. Getting as dark a suntan as possible on your summer holidays in Spain to look good when you get home.
3. Arranging to meet someone down town who you've just met in a chat room on the internet.

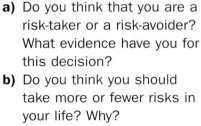

4. Getting drunk with alcohol at a party this weekend.
5. Blowing the whistle and telling on your friend who has stolen some money from someone in school.
6. Telling lies to your parents about what you are really doing at the weekend.

Activity 3 — Personal journal

a) Do you think that you are a risk-taker or a risk-avoider? What evidence have you for this decision?
b) Do you think you should take more or fewer risks in your life? Why?
c) Have you any plans to manage risk better in any specific area of your life?

Personal Development

8 HOW CAN I HANDLE EMOTIONS SAFELY?

Learning intentions

I am learning:
- ✓ to identify risks involved in expressing my emotions
- ✓ to develop strategies for expressing emotions healthily
- ✓ whether differences exist between boys and girls and how they express their emotions.

Most people go through a range of emotions each day: for example, panic because the alarm didn't go off and they slept in; or frustration when stuck in a traffic jam.

There are times when we may not feel able or comfortable about expressing our true emotions because of other people's reactions.

Activity 1 Is the risk worth taking?

a) Think of situations where you felt unable to express your true feelings. Record in a table the situation, the feeling and the risk you felt that stopped you. For example:

The situation	The feeling	The risk
When my teacher asked me if I understood the question.	Nervous and embarrassed as I didn't understand it.	That I would look stupid in front of the class and someone would make fun of me.

In groups:
b) Record all the risks that individuals identified.
c) Divide your list into three sections, 'Physical risk' (e.g. being hit), 'Emotional risk' (e.g. being laughed at) and 'Relationship risk' (e.g. losing a friend).
d) Feed back to the class and discuss the following questions:

- Which section had the most examples?
- What does this tell you about how easy it is to express our emotions?
- What happens to you when you can't express how you really feel in a situation?

There are times when it is simply not safe to express how we really feel, for example expressing your anger at a drunken person who is bothering you at a bus stop. In these situations we need to find other ways to handle our emotions that are both helpful and safe. It may be useful to use this framework to help you manage your feelings in a difficult situation:

Do something to help yourself: for example, talk to someone or do something you enjoy.

Think about ways to help yourself instead of making things worse.

Relax and take 'time out' before you act.

Accept your feelings: it's okay to feel like this.

Activity 2 — Learning to manage your feelings

a) Choose a situation from the ones you identified earlier.
b) Use the framework for managing feelings to work through the situation again.
c) Discuss with a partner how useful you think it is to use these steps.
d) Do you think the steps work for both boys and girls? If not, why not?

Boys and girls have the same feelings! But they do not always express them in the same way. What is expected by society can put a lot of pressure on how both boys and girls are 'allowed' to express their feelings.

Activity 3 — How do boys and girls express their feelings?

In groups:
a) Brainstorm situations that result in a strong feeling, for example tripping over a school bag and falling on the ground and hurting yourself.
b) Copy and complete the table below, and for each situation:

The situation	Types of feeling	Expression of feelings	Boys	Girls	Both

- record the types of feelings that could occur
- give examples of how they could be expressed
- decide who you think might express their feelings in this way, girls, boys or both?

c) Compare your information with others in your class.
d) What have you found out about feelings, their expression, and boys and girls?
e) Are there some ways of expressing feelings that are less helpful than others?
f) If so, what are they, and what would the consequences be?

Our emotional health is very important for success in our adult life. Becoming more aware of our feelings and how best to manage them when we are young will help us to grow and develop into healthier, happier adults in the future.

Activity 4 — Personal journal

a) What have you learned about how to express your emotions?
b) When is it worth taking the risk to share your emotions? Give an example.
c) When is it not worth taking the risk to share your emotions? Give an example.

Personal Development

9 HOW DO I LEARN TO TRUST?

> **Learning intentions**
>
> *I am learning:*
> - ✓ to understand what trust is and why it is vital to relationships
> - ✓ to discover what builds trust and what destroys it
> - ✓ to set goals to develop into a more trustworthy person.

A definition of trust:

'Trust is a belief that the people we depend on will do what we expect.'

Trust is one of the main building blocks of a relationship. It is the most fragile part of a relationship, because it generally takes a long time to build up, but with one careless action can be broken and destroyed.

The important characteristic of trust seems to be emotional safety, which we looked at in Topic 8. That feeling of emotional safety allows us to express our deepest feelings and fears, knowing they will be handled with care by the other person.

Now take a look at Activity 1.

 ## Activity 1 Exploring trust

As individuals:
a) How easy do you find it to trust people?
b) What is it that makes you trust someone?
c) What is it that makes you not trust someone?
d) Do you think trust is essential to relationships? Explain.

As a class:
e) Create a class list of all the things that build and destroy trust, and put it up on a chart on the wall.

Trust analysis

1 Results and Actions
I trust what you **DO**, e.g.
- You are able to do what you say.
- You are competent.
- You deliver on time.
- You produce required or expected results.
- You meet reasonable expectations.
- You are responsible for your actions.

2 Integrity and Character
I trust who you **ARE**, e.g.
- Honest in communication.
- Show commitment to me and others.
- Do what you say you will do.
- You keep everyone informed.
- Good boundaries, you share appropriately and keep confidentiality.
- You are loyal.
- Good and worthy.

3 Change and Challenges
I trust you that you will **COPE WELL** with a crisis, e.g.
- You show flexibility and perseverance.
- Resilient – able to bounce back.
- Calm and supportive under pressure.
- Don't blame or dump on others.
- You handle crisis well and are cheerful.
- You see others' points of view.
- Resourceful in handling the unknown.

4 Empathy and Care
I trust that you want what is **BEST FOR ME**, e.g.
- Helping with difficulties.
- Asking for my and other's opinions.
- Sensitive to the impact of decisions.
- Sensitive to problems.
- Fair and kind.
- Generous.
- Sharing the difficult jobs.

There are many ways to build or destroy trust. The previous table shows four main ways people trust each other (RICE). (The RICE analysis was developed by a man called Philip Merry.) When these conditions are present, trust and cooperation are built. When they are absent, trust will reduce. It is important to know that trust can deepen when you pay enough attention to build it in your relationships.

An exercise in trust

 Activity 2 How do we trust each other?

Using the four different ways to trust people outlined on page 18 (RICE), get into groups and decide which type of trusting is more important in the following types of relationships. Give reasons for your answers.

1 Mother and child

2 School classmates

3 Football team

4 Marriage partner

5 Nurse and patient

6 Politician and citizen

 **Activity 3** Personal journal

All of us tend to assume that we should be trusted automatically! So why are you worth trusting?

a) If you were to give yourself a mark in terms of a percentage, how trustworthy are you? (not trustworthy at all = 0 per cent, completely trustworthy = 100 per cent)

b) Outline your evidence to back this up.

c) In which of the four areas of trusting (RICE) are you strongest and weakest?

d) If you were to set personal goals to develop into a more trustworthy person, what goals would you set yourself?

10 HOW CAN I BECOME ASSERTIVE?

Learning intentions

I am learning:
- ✓ what it means to be assertive
- ✓ how to create win–win situations in difficult circumstances.

What does being assertive mean?

Being assertive means standing up for your rights and not being taken for granted. It also means communicating clearly what you really want, respecting your own rights and feelings and the rights and feelings of others.

Many people are not assertive for fear of displeasing others and not being liked. This may help in the short term but it could damage your relationships if failing to be assertive means you feel you are being taken for granted.

There are several different ways of being assertive.

1 Basic – a simple, straightforward expression of your beliefs, feelings or opinions using 'I want' or 'I feel'. For example:

2 Empathic – showing sensitivity, recognising feelings, but also standing up for your own rights. For example:

3 Escalating – when basic attempts have failed, you become firmer in your views, and refer to some resulting action. For example:

4 'This makes me feel' language – useful for expressing negative feelings. It involves a three-part statement:

- When you do … (describe the behaviour)
- It makes me feel … (describe the effect on you)
- Please can you … (describe what you'd prefer)

For example:

What does being aggressive mean?

Being aggressive means standing up for yourself in ways that disrespect the rights of others.

Aggressive behaviour can involve threats, name-calling, and even actual physical contact. It can also involve sarcasm, catty comments and gossip.

 ### Activity 1 Assertive or aggressive?

a) Read the statements below and decide if the person is being assertive or aggressive.

- Now look what you've made me do! My cola has spilt all over the table! Clean it up now or I'll tell Mum!
- I would really prefer you not to smoke in here as you're making me feel unwell.
- I know you wanted me to come shopping with you, but I want to get my homework done early so that I can go out later.
- If you were a real friend you would lend me the money to buy that CD.
- Give me those directions to the youth club, as you're too stupid to understand them anyway.

b) Rewrite those statements which you identified as being aggressive using assertive language. Use the 'ways of being assertive' statements to help you.

c) How will this affect how people feel and act in these situations?

It is important to remember that being assertive is about respecting yourself and others equally and allowing a win–win situation to occur. This is when both parties feel they have benefited from the situation, and one side doesn't feel they have lost out or had to give in. It's about compromise!

 ### Activity 2 Practice makes perfect

In small groups:
a) Come up with two scenarios that would require assertive behaviour for a win–win outcome. You can use the statements above to help you.
b) Role-play the situations using aggressive language.
c) Who has won and who has lost? How does it feel to lose?
d) Now re-enact the situation practising assertive language. Use any or all of the four ways of being assertive in your role-play.
e) Who has won and who has lost? How does it feel this time?
f) What makes a win–win situation? Is this always possible?

 ### Activity 3
Personal journal

a) Think of a recent situation when you were particularly aggressive towards someone, or someone was aggressive towards you. Write down a summary of what was said.
b) Were you both satisfied by the outcome of this situation?
c) Would using assertive rather than aggressive language have changed the outcome of the situation? Explain your answer.

1.1 HOW DO I DECIDE WHAT IS RIGHT OR WRONG?

> **Learning intentions**
>
> **I am learning:**
> ✓ about my moral code (deciding what is right and wrong for me and others)
> ✓ what influences my decisions about right and wrong.

Our morals are our beliefs about what is right or wrong. These beliefs are often formed by our religion, society, political point of view, the community we live in, our culture and family background.

All of these things contribute to our personal moral code, which determines our individual behaviour in different circumstances. This moral code can result in conflicts both personally and with others when working out what is right or wrong.

Activity 1 Deciding what is right or wrong

a) Below are seven actions for you to sort as right or wrong. Make two columns and decide where you'd put each of the actions.

■ Smacking children

■ Copying homework

■ Not putting litter in the bin

■ Reporting bullying

■ Giving an elderly person your seat

■ Always telling the truth

■ Stealing from a supermarket

b) What influenced your decisions on right or wrong?
c) Compare your list with a partner and then a group of four. Are all the lists the same? If not, why not?
d) How do the differences between the lists make it difficult to make an overall decision about right and wrong?

We don't all make the same choices, because the factors that influence our choices are different for each individual. The decisions we make about what is right or wrong, based on the influences in our lives, are what is called our 'moral code'. This is a very difficult thing to define, and we often only discover our true morals when they are challenged and we experience a moral dilemma.

Activity 2 Exploring my moral code

a) Read the story below, which describes a moral dilemma.

Brian and Jenny have been best friends since primary school. It's the summer holidays and the pair have met up in town, outside Tesco. Brian bounds up to Jenny and hands her a big bag of luxury chocolates. He pulls another bag from under his jacket and proceeds to stuff a few into his mouth.

'Where did you get the money for these? You told me you were broke!' says Jenny.

Brian laughs nervously. 'I nicked them! Tesco make such huge profits every day, they're not going to miss a few bags of sweets!'

Just at that moment, Brian's mum walks out of Tesco with her weekly shopping. Things have been hard for Brian's family since his dad was made redundant.

'Hello, you two! Brian, where did you get the money for those sweets? You told me you had none yesterday!'

Brian looked his mother straight in the face and said, 'Jenny bought them.'

Brian's mum looked at Jenny: 'You really shouldn't buy him sweets. He needs to learn to budget his money and not spend his friends' money too. How much were they, and I'll pay you back. Have you got the receipt?'

In groups:
b) Discuss the following questions:

- What are Jenny's options, and what would be the consequences of each option?
- How do you think Jenny is feeling, faced with these dilemmas?
- What are the possible consequences of never lying?
- What are the possible consequences of assuming that lying is okay?

c) Complete the ending of the story using your discussion and the statements below to help you decide on a resolution.

- You should never lie.
- It's okay to lie so that someone doesn't get hurt.
- It's okay to lie so that someone doesn't get into trouble.
- It's okay to lie if you won't get what you want by being honest.
- There's nothing wrong with lying if you want to, regardless of the reason.

Activity 3 Personal journal

Everyone has done things they have felt guilty about and regret their actions.

a) Write down an example of something you have done which resulted in you feeling guilty.
b) Why did you feel guilty?
c) What was the moral code and how did you break it?

12 HOW CAN I LEARN FROM MISTAKES?

Learning intentions

I am learning:
- ✓ about how I respond to making mistakes
- ✓ that making mistakes can result in a positive outcome.

For many of us, how we view mistakes says a lot about our personality and attitude to life and learning.

Situation

Your class have just got their papers back from an end-of-topic test. Two students scored 43 per cent.

Student A thinks:

I'm stupid, I can't do this subject.

She feels defeated, angry and helpless and throws the paper in the bin.

Student B resolves:

I know I can do better than this! I'll speak to Mr Jones later and get some pointers for next time.

He feels determined and motivated to do better next time.

Activity 1
Are mistakes a problem or an opportunity?

a) Consider the situation provided. What can you conclude about the attitudes of students A and B to making mistakes?

b) Which student is going to benefit from getting a score of 43 per cent? Give reasons for your choice.

c) Think about your own reaction to making mistakes. Would you tend to be more like student A or B?

d) How has your own reaction to making mistakes affected your ability to learn?

'I've never made a mistake, I've only learnt from experience.'

Thomas A. Edison, American inventor

'The man who makes no mistakes does not usually make anything.'

William Connor Magee, Irish clergyman

'Anyone who doesn't make mistakes isn't trying hard enough.'

Wess Roberts, author

'Mistakes are part of the dues one pays for a full life.'

Sophia Loren, film actress

There are lots of inspirational quotes on the topic of making mistakes, as shown on the opposite page.

All of these quotes suggest that part of the learning process derives from making mistakes. It is only by doing so that we learn what to do – and, importantly, what not to do – next time.

Thomas J. Watson, American businessman and President of IBM, has this to say about success:

> 'Would you like me to give you a formula for success? It's quite simple, really: double your rate of failure. You're thinking of failure as the enemy of success, but it isn't at all. You can be discouraged by failure – or you can learn from it. So go ahead and make mistakes. Make all you can. Because, remember, that's where you'll find success. On the far side.'

Thomas J. Watson, President of IBM

Activity 2 Learning from my mistakes

a) Reflect on a mistake you have made. This can be in any context, not necessarily linked to school. Use the headings below to record your thoughts, feelings, actions and outcomes from making your mistake.

Description of the mistake	What I thought	What I felt	What I did	What happened as a result

b) In the light of the messages from the quotes in this topic, can you suggest how you could have behaved differently?

c) If you were to change your thinking around the mistake, making it more positive, how would this impact on your feelings, actions and outcomes?

It is rather comforting to realise that everyone makes mistakes and that very often the bigger the mistake, the more we can learn.

Activity 3 Personal journal

Some mistakes can have very serious consequences, and it is better that we try not to make them at all! In your journal:

- Think of a mistake that someone may not get the opportunity to learn from.
- How could innocent bystanders and their families be affected by the mistakes of others?
- What could people do to avoid these kinds of mistakes?

13 WHY DO WE USE DRUGS?

> **Learning intentions**
>
> *I am learning:*
> - ✓ about the medical and non-medical use of drugs
> - ✓ about the effects of drugs and the personal problems drugs can cause
> - ✓ to identify what might motivate someone to use drugs.

What automatically springs into your mind when someone says the word 'drugs'? Perhaps you think about cannabis use, or young people taking 'ecstasy' at a party? Drugs certainly seem to have got a very bad name. However, without drugs many of us would never have survived birth or the first few years of our life. Many people would be suffering terrible pain, and our life expectancy would be considerably lower.

The most significant use of drugs in our society is for medical purposes. We all use them to some degree to help ease pain, treat infections or control medical conditions such as diabetes or high blood pressure.

 Activity 1 Investigating the medical use of drugs

a) Choose one of the questions below to answer by carrying out some research.

- ■ 'If a drug is used for medical purposes, does that mean it is safe?'
- ■ 'Can medical drugs be misused or abused?'
- ■ 'Can medical drugs be misused for recreational purposes?'

b) Present your research to the class. You could present it using PowerPoint, a poster, a role-play, video etc. Be prepared to answer questions about your presentation.

c) Reflect on what you have learned from your own and others' research. Record points of interest in your personal journal.

So what does the word 'drug' actually mean?

> *The term 'drug' can be defined as 'any substance which, when taken, has the effect of altering the way the body works or the way a person behaves, feels, sees or thinks'.*
>
> (Taken from Drugs: Guidance for Schools in Northern Ireland, 2004)

It should be clear from your research so far that there are a variety of drugs used for recreational purposes, and that their use has a variety of effects and consequences. Some of these may be positive: feeling more relaxed, happy, energetic and confident. Some could be extremely negative: feeling scared, unable to sleep, vomiting, paranoia, getting a criminal record, and even coma or death.

Not all drugs cause problems. Many people can use drugs throughout their life with no identifiable problems at all. Others, however, develop significant problems as a result of drug use.

Activity 2 Recreational use of drugs

Look at the photos of a range of substances that all have an effect on how a person behaves, feels, sees and thinks. Use other sources of information to help you answer the questions overleaf.

Magic mushrooms

Alcohol　　**Gas lighter fluid**　　**Coffee**　　**Nail polish**

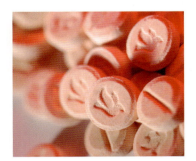

Ecstasy　　**Cannabis**　　**Tea**

Chocolate　　**Cigarettes**　　**Paracetamol**

Personal Development

27

13 WHY DO WE USE DRUGS? *CONTINUED*

Activity 2 Recreational use of drugs *continued*

Having considered all the photos on page 27, complete the following activities.

In pairs:
a) Divide the substances into two groups: legal and illegal substances.
b) Add at least two more substances to each list.
c) How does each substance in the photos alter 'the way the body works, or the way a person behaves, feels, sees or thinks'?
d) Create a new table and label it 'consequences' like the one below. Record **all** the possible consequences, positive and negative, that would result from taking each substance.

Substance	Consequence	
	Positive	Negative
Paracetamol		

e) On the basis of your information, rank the substances in order of risk.

Activity 3 Tackling problems caused by drugs

In groups:
a) Imagine you are a local political party with the task of tackling the problems caused by drug use.
b) What problems in your community are linked to drug use?
c) Make a list of the possible actions you could take and what problems they would address.
d) What other agencies could help you tackle some of the identified problems?

e) There are financial cutbacks in public spending and you are told you will have to cut your planned work by half.

- What would you consider to be the most important action you have to undertake in tackling drug problems?
- Write a proposal to take to the local council outlining your revised plans, giving reasons for your choice.

Drugs do cause many people lots of problems, which can have far-reaching consequences. Yet many people still choose to take them anyway. So what motivates people to start using drugs, and to continue using them even if problems start to occur?

Motivation broadly falls into three categories:

1 to fit in
2 to deal with pain
3 to find pleasure.

Activity 4 What motivates people to use drugs?

a) Using the three categories above to help you, suggest reasons why young people use drugs (other than for medical reasons).

In groups of four:
b) Consider all the reasons and create a list.
c) Can you suggest alternative activities that would not involve the use of drugs but would help satisfy the motivators listed above?

Activity 5 Personal journal

Having explored all the problems caused by drugs, you will realise that motivation to use drugs must become very strong to over-ride these.

a) What are the good reasons for using drugs? Record your ideas in your journal.
b) What are the bad reasons for using drugs? Record some examples.
c) Should you always respond to your motivations? Why or why not?

Fitting in

Dealing with pain

Finding pleasure

14 WHAT IS ADDICTION?

Learning intentions

I am learning:
- what the term addiction means
- about the difficulty of breaking an addictive habit
- about attitudes towards addiction.

Addiction is a very complex problem that affects not only the physical and mental health of individuals, but also their families and society.

What do you understand by the term 'addiction'?

 ## Activity 1 Understanding addiction

In groups:
a) Discuss and come up with a definition for 'addiction'.
b) Compare your definition with other groups in the class, and come to a class-agreed definition.

In pairs:
c) Brainstorm a list of all the things you think it is possible to become addicted to. Come together to create a class list.
d) Design a poster/display to explain what addiction means, what could trigger it, and what things can be addictive.

Many definitions of addiction are extremely scientific and difficult to understand, so here is a simplified version:

- An addiction is any thinking or behaviour that is habit forming, repetitive and difficult or impossible to control.
- Usually the addiction brings short-term pleasure, but there may be long-term consequences in terms of an individual's health and welfare.
- Addictions tend to steadily take more control and power over the person. With many addictions, the control is both psychological (the mind tells them they need it and can't live without it) and physical (the body has adjusted to having the drug and now reacts when it is not there).

 ## Activity 2 How easy is it to give up smoking?

You are going to design and carry out a survey of smokers and ex-smokers. You will need to consider the following points.

- How will you identify the people? Will they be staff in school, parents, relatives, friends etc?
- How many people do you need, to get accurate results?
- How will you gather the information? Will you ask questions and record their answers, or will you ask them to fill out a survey sheet?

- How will you represent the information: written, illustrated, graphs, diagrams etc?
- How will you present your findings to the class?
- What conclusions and recommendations can you make using your evidence?

In groups of four:

Design your survey sheet around the following questions. You can amend them or add others if you wish. Leave enough space to record the answers!

- Are you a smoker or ex-smoker?
- Have you tried to give up smoking?
- What motivated you to try and give up?
- How many times have you tried to give up?
- What happened that caused you to fail?
- How did you achieve success?
- What symptoms did you have?
- Did these symptoms change over time, and if so in what way?
- Do you still get the urge to smoke?
- What triggers these urges?

Activity 3 Class debate around issues of addiction

You can do this activity as an agree/disagree line debate, moving up and down the line according to your answers to each question.

Or

You can get into groups and argue for or against the statements, swapping over your standpoint so that sometimes you argue for a statement and sometimes against it.

Use the selection of statements below, or make up some of your own for the debate.

- 'My addiction made me do it!'
- Bad behaviour can be excused if the person is an addict.
- A person should be able to snap out of it! Addiction is all in the mind.
- Breaking an addiction is all down to willpower.
- Addiction is a recognised illness and should be treated accordingly.
- Addicts need help, not criticism.
- Smokers should not be allowed any surgery on the National Health Service, as their illness is self-inflicted.

Activity 4 Personal journal

Think about what you have learned in this topic.

a) What important facts have you learned about addiction?
b) How has this influenced your attitude towards addicts and addiction?
c) Who is responsible for addiction to drugs?

15 WHAT IS EQUALITY?

Learning intentions

I am learning:
- to explain what is meant by 'equality'
- to give examples of some groups in our society who may be treated unfairly.

This part of your book will help you to investigate 'equality and social justice', one of the key themes of Local and Global Citizenship. The next seven topics look at the issue of 'equality'. The following activities will help you understand what this word means.

 Activity 1 A 'level playing field'?

Read the article below.

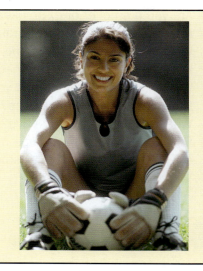

From now on there's going to be a level playing field, literally. Despite success in youth teams across the UK, girls over 11 have been banned from playing in boys' teams. Now the ban is to be lifted. The Football Association has responded to an outcry from female players and MPs after a campaign by an 11-year-old defender with a London youth team who was told she would be thrown out of her club on her 12th birthday.

Minnie Cruttwell, the only girl to play with Balham Blazers, was so angry she wrote to Tessa Jowell, the Secretary of State for Culture, Media and Sport to challenge the rule. Ms Jowell intervened, and after an extensive consultation, the FA decided to review the ban and has drawn up proposals to allow teenage girls to play.

Adapted from *Independent on Sunday*, 27 May 2007

In pairs, answer the following questions:
a) What did Minnie think was unfair in this situation?
b) What does the article mean when it talks about a 'level playing field'?
c) Why do you think the FA decided to review its ban?
d) Do you think the FA is right to allow teenage girls to play soccer in a boys' team? Why?

Everyone is entitled to all their human rights no matter what their race, colour, gender, language, religion, political or other opinion, nationality, or social status.

UDHR Article 2

In this example a decision was taken to make sure that girls and boys were treated equally. Equality is about ensuring that everyone is treated fairly, regardless of who they are or what groups they may belong to. In 1948 the governments of the world signed the Universal Declaration of Human Rights (UDHR) promising to protect everyone's human rights. One of the promises they made is shown on the left.

However, even though equality is a human right there are still groups of people who are treated unfairly. The next activity will help you to think about these equality issues.

Activity 2 Dreaming of an equal world …

a) Read the quotation below. What equality issue was Martin Luther King Jnr. talking about?
b) Write down examples of other groups of people who you think are sometimes treated unfairly. Think about what you have heard on the news or your own experiences to help you.
c) Now write your own version of Dr King's speech including all these groups.

> 'I have a dream that my four little children will one day live in a nation where they will not be judged by the colour of their skin but by the content of their character … I have a dream that … one day right there in Alabama little black boys and black girls will be able to join hands with little white boys and white girls as sisters and brothers … I have a dream today!'
> Martin Luther King Jnr., 28 August 1963, Washington, DC

 ## Activity 3 What is equality?

a) Write out the Martin Luther King quote and time yourself to see how long it takes you. Ask a partner to check it for neatness, accuracy and speed. Award a mark out of ten for each of these.
b) Now you are going to repeat the exercise, but this time everyone is going to be treated the same. So everyone must write with their left hand and no one is allowed to wear glasses.
c) Compare times and scores.
d) As a class, discuss:

- How easy was this exercise the first time compared with the second time?
- How many people did better the first time?
- If this were a real test how would it feel?
- Is treating everyone the same the same as treating everyone fairly?

Equality is more than just treating people the same. Sometimes it means treating people differently so that they have the same chances as everyone else.

Local and Global Citizenship

33

16 WHAT CAUSES DISCRIMINATION?

Learning intentions

I am learning:
- ✓ to explain the differences between prejudice, stereotyping and discrimination
- ✓ to work with others to investigate connections between harmful attitudes and actions.

RACE ATTACKS ON THE INCREASE

New study shows women get paid less than men

Police say attack on youths was sectarian

These headlines show that some people in Northern Ireland face prejudice because of the group they belong to. In Book 1 you learned that there are connections between prejudice, stereotypes and discrimination:

- a stereotype is a generalisation about a group of people that isn't altogether true, e.g. 'all teenage boys are thugs'
- prejudice is making judgements about people (pre-judging) based on stereotypes, e.g. 'Stay away from those boys in the park, they're bound to be thugs'
- discrimination is taking unfair action against someone because of the group they belong to, e.g. 'no teenage boys are allowed in this shop'.

Activity 1 Sort them out!

a) Read the statements A–J and decide if they are examples of stereotypes, prejudices or discrimination.

A All foreigners can't speak our language.

B All gay people have AIDS.

C Our firm does not employ migrant workers.

D Women don't work as hard as men.

E Migrant workers are not welcome here.

F Young people cannot be trusted.

G Our school refuses to accept people who are disabled.

H People with young children need not apply.

I The Chinese have nothing to offer our community.

J We don't serve Travellers.

b) Now copy and complete the table (one has been done for you). Some statements may fit in more than one column!

Prejudice	Discrimination	Stereotyping
	C Our firm does not employ migrant workers.	

Activity 2 From attitudes to actions

a) At the furthest ends of a wall in your classroom, place two signs: 'Attitude' and 'Action'.
b) On cards copy the statements A–J.

As a class:
c) Discuss where to place each of these cards on your spectrum from Attitude to Action.
d) Look at the statements at the 'Attitude' end and discuss how these negative attitudes could lead people to take negative actions.
e) What do you think is more harmful, 'negative attitudes' or 'negative actions'?

Now you have an understanding of the differences between prejudice, stereotyping and discrimination and have thought about these in terms of attitudes and actions, read the article on the right and complete the activity below.

Activity 3 Is discrimination a problem for our society?

In groups of four:
a) Copy the following statements onto separate pieces of paper and fold them up:

- Is discrimination a problem for our society?
- Are attitudes just as harmful as actions?
- Do we treat migrant workers fairly?
- Can harmful attitudes lead to harmful actions?

b) Mix these up and select one each in your group. Your challenge is to speak about your chosen title for a full minute. The rules are: *no hesitation, no deviation (going off the point) and no repetition.*
c) Use the information in the article to help. Have a vote at the end and elect a winner for your group.

Female migrant workers experience widespread mistreatment

Female migrant workers are experiencing widespread discrimination and mistreatment in the workplace, according to a study being published by the Equality Authority today. The research says they have experienced under-payment or non-payment of wages, unethical recruitment practices and breaches of their entitlement to a contract, as well as harassment by employers. It also says many are working in jobs below their skills level, with some of the women employed as cleaners or housekeepers despite having university degrees. Some of the women involved say they believed Irish employees would never be treated the way they are.

(*Belfast Telegraph*, Monday 6 November 2006)

17 WHAT ARE THE DIFFERENT TYPES OF DISCRIMINATION?

Learning intentions

I am learning:
- to understand the different ways that organisations and institutions may discriminate against certain groups in our society
- to explain what is meant by the term 'discrimination'.

In the last topic you discovered that discrimination means acting negatively towards people, often through prejudice. *Individuals* can act in a discriminatory way towards others when they harass or treat other individuals badly because of who they are. Do you remember in Book 1 that you learned about how people can act in sectarian or racist ways towards each other? There are laws to try to prevent this. For example, if someone attacks an individual because they are from a different ethnic group they could be convicted of a racist crime. You will learn more about how our society deals with such crimes in Book 3. In this topic, you will find out about what happens when people who run organisations and institutions (like businesses, schools, shops or government departments) allow their prejudices to affect who they offer jobs to, or who they promote, or who they allow to buy things etc. They may not be physically attacking people, but they may be preventing them from having the same chances as everyone else – and that is what the law calls 'discrimination'. This type of discrimination usually happens around issues to do with employment or access to 'goods and services'.

The next activity will help you to think about which groups of people are more vulnerable when it comes to discrimination, and also help you to think about examples of different types of discrimination.

Activity 1 How easy is it for me … ?

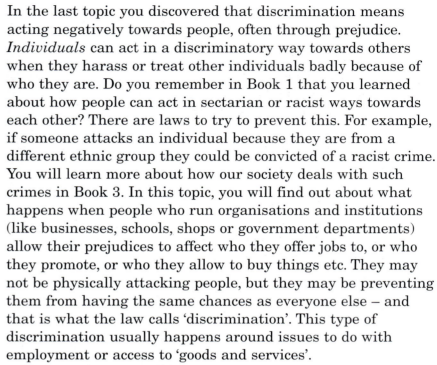

In small groups:

a) Look at the individuals on the left and carry out the quiz (on page 37) for each of them – decide on a score for each of the ten actions, and add up the total for each person. (There are no right or wrong answers.)

- Paul is a 24-year-old wheelchair user. He has severe learning disabilities and needs constant help from a carer.
- Sasha is a 45-year-old migrant worker. She has difficulty speaking English and struggles to find work. When she does, it is very poorly paid.
- Margaret is a 45-year-old ex-prisoner. She has been out of work since leaving prison.
- George is a 30-year-old member of the Travelling community.

QUIZ
1. I can afford to live in a good house.
2. I can have an active social life.
3. I can get on and off buses easily.
4. I can make my way around the town centre easily and without help.
5. I can use public toilets even if access requires the use of steps.
6. I can get served in any shop.
7. I can go to my doctor and discuss issues that relate to my health and well-being.
8. I can get a job or get promotion as easily as anyone else.
9. I can open a bank account or take out a library card.
10. I can use my education to get a good job.

SCORING

A	Easily	5
B	With slight difficulty	3
C	With moderate difficulty	2
D	With lots of difficulty	1

b) Feed back your scores and reasoning to the rest of the class. Did other groups have different scores? Why?

As a class:

c) Try to list as many examples of how organisations may discriminate against certain groups as you can. You can use the examples above and any other ideas you have.

d) Now try to group these together. Which examples are connected to employment? Which are connected to access to 'goods and services'?

Discrimination is ...

Examples of discrimination include ...

There are different ways that organisations or institutions may discriminate against people. Some of these are very obvious. For example, if a business decides to only employ white people it's quite clear that they are discriminating against people from other ethnic groups. Some types of discrimination are less obvious. For example, if a shop doesn't have a wheelchair ramp the owner is making it more difficult for a wheelchair user to have the same chance as others to buy the goods in the shop.

Activity 2
Personal journal

In the last topic you were given a simple definition of the word 'discrimination'. Use what you have learned so far in this topic to expand this definition and explain as fully as you can what the term means.

18 HOW DOES THE LAW PROTECT PEOPLE FROM DISCRIMINATION?

Learning intentions
I am learning:
- to identify the groups protected by Section 75 of the Northern Ireland Act
- about how some organisations have to make sure they promote equality for all.

As you discovered in the last topic, some groups in society can be more vulnerable than others to being treated unfairly. To make sure that people are protected from this, governments can make laws and take action against organisations and institutions that discriminate against people because of the group they belong to. There are many of these laws in Northern Ireland and you will find out more about them in the next topic. In this topic you will find out about one of our most important pieces of equality law.

Following the Good Friday/Belfast Agreement, the government set out in law that, as well as discrimination being illegal, government organisations and other public bodies (such as hospitals and universities) also have to take active steps to make sure that certain groups in our society have access to exactly the same opportunities as everyone else. This law is written down in Section 75 of the Northern Ireland Act (1998).

Northern Ireland Act (1998) Section 75

Public bodies must promote equality of opportunity between the following groups. This means that they must make sure that everyone is given the same chance as everyone else regardless of …

 Activity 1 What groups are protected by 'Section 75'?

a) Read the information on the left. It is the start of 'Section 75' of the Northern Ireland Act – but the bottom half is missing. It has been ripped off!

1 … religious belief
2 … political opinion
3 … class backgrounds, e.g. working class, middle class etc.
4 … age
5 … ethnic group
6 … job
7 … sexual orientation
8 … gender
9 … whether they have disabilities or not
10 … whether they drive cars or not

Local and Global Citizenship

11 ... whether they have been in prison or not

12 ... whether they have dependants (i.e. children, older relatives or other people they need to look after) or not

13 ... whether they play sports or not   **14** ... whether they are married or not

b) Now look at the strips of paper. Nine of these strips of paper belong to the actual law. In pairs, decide which nine are correct and write them down.
c) Look at the answers on page 90.
d) As a class, discuss the following:

- Why do you think these nine groups of people are listed in Section 75?
- Do you think any groups that should have been in have been left out? If so, which and why?

Activity 2 An equality 'policy'

In groups:
a) Choose one of the following public bodies or organisations and imagine that you are the 'bosses': a university; a hospital; the police service; a government department.
b) Your task is to produce an 'equality policy' for your organisation. This means that you have to write down exactly how you are going to make sure that everyone mentioned in Section 75 would be given the same chances if they came into contact with your organisation. To help you do this, discuss each of the following questions:

- How will you make sure that you employ people fairly?
- What about holiday leave for employees, sick leave etc? Are there any groups of people you might need to make special arrangements for?
- How will you make sure that people who work for you don't harrass or upset others because of the group they belong to?
- Will you have rules around how your employees treat members of the public?

Write down your answers, starting each with: 'We will make sure that ...'

c) Now present your 'policy' to the rest of the class. You might want to give your organisation a name for this presentation!
d) The rest of the class should ask you questions to make sure that your 'policy' promotes equality for *all* of the Section 75 groups. When they are asking questions they should pretend to be someone from one of these groups. For example, they might say: 'I am a young person: if I had a complaint about your organisation, how would you make sure my views were taken seriously?', or 'I am a member of a political party: how would you make sure our views are adequately represented?'
e) Now make any changes you need to your policy.
f) Use your ICT skills to produce a finished copy of your organisation's 'equality policy' for display.

19 WHAT IS THE ROLE OF THE EQUALITY COMMISSION?

Learning intentions

I am learning:
- to understand the role of the law in equality cases
- to evaluate scenarios from an equality perspective.

One of the roles of Northern Ireland's Equality Commission is to advise people who feel they are the victims of discrimination in equality issues. In Northern Ireland the following legislation is important in equality cases:

- Disability Discrimination Act 1995
- Equality (Disability, etc.) (Northern Ireland) Order 2000
- Equal Pay Act (Northern Ireland) 1970 (amended 1984, 2004)
- Employment Equality (Age) Regulations (Northern Ireland) 2006
- Fair Employment and Treatment (Northern Ireland) Order 1998
- Race Relations (Northern Ireland) Order 1997 (amended 2003)
- Sex Discrimination (Northern Ireland) Order 1976 (amended 1988, 2001, 2005)
- Northern Ireland Act 1998 (Section 75)

Activity 1 Who is protected by equality law?

In pairs:

a) Ask your teacher to allocate one piece of legislation to each couple. Using the internet and the websites for the Equality Commission (www.equalityni.org), Office of the First and Deputy First Minister (www.ofmdfmni.gov.uk/index.htm) and Google (www.google.co.uk), prepare in up to three sentences a summary of *who* this legislation is meant to protect.

b) Then join with another pair who have researched the same piece of legislation and share your answer. Get a volunteer from each group of four to report to the rest of the class.

c) Write the key findings for each piece of legislation on a flipchart sheet and stick on the wall. Use this information to help you with Activity 2.

Activity 2 What are equality issues?

a) Read the following 'complaints'.

> The best qualified and most experienced person was not appointed for a job because they were 'too old' and 'would not be able to do the job quickly enough'.

> A school that only has female pupils appoints a female PE teacher over better qualified males.

> A Christian school which receives public funding refuses to employ non-Christians.

> An Asian man was not considered for a job on the grounds of his ethnicity.

> A disabled person is denied a job in the armed forces.

> A public bar refuses to serve drink to members of the Travelling community.

> A public authority refuses to allow women with children to apply for promotion.

> A government department refuses to employ homosexuals.

In pairs:

b) Using what you have learned so far:
- identify the equality issue that is raised in each case
- try to match the complaint to any of the legislation above and decide whether any of the lquality legislation might apply (not all the complaints are protected by the legislation)
- come to a conclusion as to the advice you would give the person complaining – do they have a case or not?

c) Feed back to the rest of the class.

Activity 3
Ask the experts

As a class:
Review the last activity. Were there scenarios where you couldn't decide if the equality legislation applied? Either write a letter to the Equality Commission or invite a guest speaker to come and talk to you about the scenario you have chosen. For example, a trade unionist, a personnel manager, an employer, someone from OFMDFM or the Equality Commission, or maybe even your Principal might help you deepen your understanding.

Divide your class into groups that will organise: invitations, hospitality, room requirements, questions, publicity, a chairperson for the session, thanking the visitor etc. You might like to ask your expert their views on some of the scenarios above.

Local and Global Citizenship

20 HOW CAN WE PROMOTE EQUALITY?

Learning intentions

I am learning:
✓ to measure how effectively my school values equality
✓ how to challenge harmful attitudes or behaviours appropriately.

As you have been learning, not everyone in our society is able to share the advantages it has to offer. Many migrant workers, for example, have difficulties when they become ill due to difficulties with speaking English. In turn, healthcare providers offer the services of interpreters to address this issue. As a starting point, it might be useful for you to look at your own school to see what it does to promote equality.

 Activity 1 What is my school doing to promote equality?

Working in groups, carry out an audit of how effectively your school promotes equality so that you can complete an 'Equality Footprint' for your school.

a) Copy and complete the grid below. Discuss the evidence you come up with before you reach a verdict on whether each criterion is met or not.

b) Now draw a giant footprint with six ripples, as in the illustration. For every two equality indicators that your school meets, colour one ripple from the centre out. The bigger the footprint the bigger the impact these indicators have on your school community.

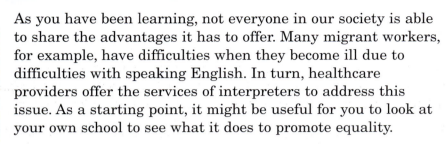

Equality indicators Our school …	Evidence	Met (Yes/No)
1 Welcomes people of all religious beliefs		
2 Is tolerant of people of all sexual orientation		
3 Has equality-related statements in its prospectus		
4 Has a policy on bullying and hurtful behaviour		
5 Has a policy and a designated teacher for helping pupils with special needs		
6 Offers special help in classes to those who may be disadvantaged		
7 Provides disabled access to all parts of the school		
8 Accepts a wide range of democratic political opinions		
9 Provides a curriculum that is fair and inclusive for all		
10 Offers activities to promote good community relations		
11 Listens to pupils and takes account of their views		
12 Offers opportunities for everyone to celebrate diversity		

c) Share and discuss your 'Equality Footprint' with the rest of the class.

Activity 2 Could we do more to promote equality?

Do you think your school is doing enough to promote equality, or could it do more? Using your findings from Activity 1 and any other relevant information, prepare a short report that could be sent to your school council or to the board of governors with your findings and any suggestions that you might have.

There are many other organisations that play a part in trying to promote equality. One method they use is posters which can help to change attitudes about issues. Look at the posters here and complete Activity 3.

**A Racism free zone
(Source: Equality Authority)**

**B Career down a different path
(Source: The Equality Commission
for Northern Ireland)**

**C Labelling by age isn't on
(Source: The Equality Commission
for Northern Ireland)**

 ## Activity 3 How can we promote equality?

In pairs:

a) Discuss each of the posters:

- What point is being made?
- What methods does it use to get across its point?
- How effective do you think it is?

b) Decide on an equality issue that is important to you and design a postcard. Think about the issue, the harmful attitude or behaviour that you wish to challenge and the way you will get this message across, e.g. use of puns, catchy slogan, images, colour etc. Refer back to the posters' techniques. When everybody in the class has created their own postcard, place these on a wall in the classroom in order to create one really huge equality collage.

**D Do you stereotype?
(Source: Equality Commission for
Northern Ireland/Anthony Bergin
Aquinas Grammar School Belfast)**

21 HOW DO NGOS PROMOTE EQUALITY?

Learning intentions

I am learning:
- ✓ to understand what a Non-Governmental Organisation does
- ✓ to reflect on and evaluate what I have learned.

The letters NGO stand for Non-Governmental Organisation. This means they are not funded by the government and operate independently.

One role of NGOs is advocacy. This means speaking up for and working on behalf of particular groups by challenging governments, providing aid and relief, giving advice etc.

 Activity 1 What does an NGO do?

In pairs:

a) Match each logo with its name and description. Each image should give you clues about its meaning, so write down what messages you think each logo suggests; look closely at the colours, designs, shapes and sizes.

b) Report back to the class.

Age Concern is the UK's largest organisation working for and with older people. Age Concern's work ranges from providing vital local services to influencing public opinion and government. Every day they are in touch with thousands of older people from all kinds of backgrounds – enabling them to make more of life.

One Parent Families | Gingerbread believes we can build a fairer society for all families, in which lone parents and their children are not disadvantaged and do not suffer from poverty, isolation or social exclusion.

Disability Action works to make sure that people with disabilities have their full rights as citizens. They work for inclusion and try to influence the decisions government makes. They also work to change attitudes about the disabled.

The Chinese Welfare Association works to secure the future of the Chinese community in Northern Ireland. It works for racial equality, and aims to help all sections of the community to participate fully in both the development of the community and the wider society.

Local and Global Citizenship

44

Activity 2 How do NGOs promote equality?

In groups:

a) Choose an 'equality' NGO that interests you and research it on the internet. You can choose one of the organisations from Activity 1 or go to the Equality Commission website (www.equalityni.org), find their 'links' section and search the wide range of NGOs in Northern Ireland that work for equality.

b) Your research should cover the following:

- the history and background of the NGO
- the work they do
- the activities/events they have organised
- how they are funded
- how the public can help (besides fund-raising)
- anything else you think that is interesting or important, e.g. why you think the work they are involved in is significant.

c) Decide how to present your findings. You could choose a PowerPoint presentation, a report, a poster, or web page etc. Whichever approach you select, you must make use of ICT.

 ## Activity 3 Am I enjoying my learning?

a) Produce a class dartboard, labelled as in the illustration.
b) Think about your learning and decide how much you are enjoying it.
c) Everyone writes their initials in the ring that is appropriate to them.
d) As a class discuss the following questions:

- What are the most important things you are learning about equality?
- What things have surprised or shocked you?
- Have all your questions been answered?
- If not, what can you still do about this?

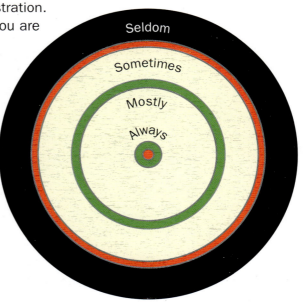

Local and Global Citizenship

22 WHAT IS SOCIAL JUSTICE?

> **Learning intentions**
>
> *I am learning:*
> ✓ how people can be excluded from society because of their material circumstances
> ✓ to define the term 'social justice'.

In Topics 15–21 you learned about equality. In particular you looked at how some people may be treated unfairly simply because of the groups they belong to. In Topics 22–29 you will find out other ways in which inequality can arise in society, by exploring how some people are excluded from society because of their 'material circumstances' (the conditions they find themselves living in).

Most of us have been given a lot of opportunities in our lives and have used these opportunities to develop our potential. Our need to feel good about ourselves and have a sense of belonging are to some extent being met by the things we do, our family and our friends. Abraham Maslow was a psychologist who thought that people developed as their needs were met. His pyramid summarises his ideas, showing the five levels of human need. The most basic needs are at the bottom. The most complex needs are at the top. Maslow believed that once people had their survival needs met they would develop by trying to ensure that their safety needs were met, and then their social needs etc. So if people's basic needs are not met then they cannot develop any further and cannot reach their full potential.

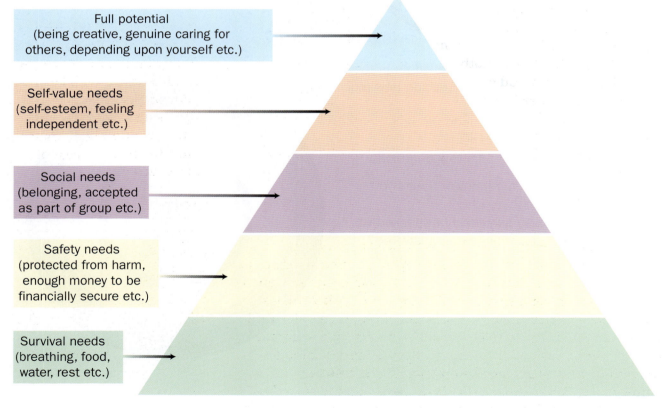

Maslow's pyramid of need

Activity 1 Meeting basic needs

a) In your group read each factfile below and decide where on Maslow's pyramid you would place each person.

b) Discuss what could be done to help each person reach their fullest human potential, and record your ideas under the following headings:
- What the person themselves could do
- What society could do
- What the government could do

c) Share your ideas with the rest of the class and then discuss the following questions:
- Whose responsibility is it to help individuals develop?
- Who can make the biggest difference in terms of helping people meet their full potential: the individual themselves, society as a whole or the government?

Charlie is 17 years old and is homeless. She sleeps in a shelter some nights but mostly sleeps outside. She has no family and has to beg so she can buy food. Most days she only has one basic meal.

Jim is 11 and feels left out in school. He's dreading 'non-uniform day' – his classmates will make fun of him because he doesn't have the latest football top. His mum and dad can't afford it. The other kids all talk about their holidays in America and France; he feels isolated because his family can't afford trips.

Margaret is 87 and lives on her own. She has no family and most of her old friends have died. Her pension just about covers her food and electric bills but in winter she finds it hard to cover the cost of her heating too.

Some people think that if individuals' needs are not met in a society then the society cannot develop either. Social justice is about making sure that *everyone*'s most basic needs are met so that they are given a chance to develop *equally*. It involves meeting people's survival needs, by providing them with food, shelter and health care. But it is also about giving everyone equal chances to develop to their fullest potential through providing them with a good education and access to employment. Most importantly it involves making sure that *governments* provide these things for all their citizens equally.

23 WHAT IS POVERTY?

Learning intentions

I am learning:
- to explain what is meant by 'absolute poverty'
- to evaluate some of the reasons given for the causes of poverty in developing countries.

In the last topic you learned that social justice was about making sure everyone had their basic needs met equally. Unfortunately we do not live in an equal world or even in an equal society. In this topic you will discover some facts and figures about global inequalities and begin to understand the nature of poverty, its causes and consequences.

 Activity 1 The truth about absolute poverty

a) Read these statements and decide which ones are true or false.

1. There are 1 million homeless people in the world.
2. 50 per cent of the world's population live on less than $2 a day.
3. Three million people in the world cannot read a book or write their own name.
4. 25 per cent of the people in the world don't have safe drinking water.
5. One million children die each year from diseases that could have been prevented by simple vaccines.

b) Now check the answers on page 90.

As a class:
c) Discuss which facts surprised you.
d) Record the accurate facts on a spidergram.

You can see from these basic facts that poverty affects people's health, access to education and to shelter. The World Bank says that people living on less than a $1 a day are living in 'absolute poverty' and people living on less than $2 a day are living in 'moderate poverty'. If we use this as a guide then the following countries are amongst the poorest in the world: Afghanistan, Bangladesh, Burkina Faso, Ethiopia, Rwanda and Uganda. These countries are sometimes called 'third world' countries but it's more usual to call them 'developing countries'.

Different people give different explanations for why we live in such an unequal world (see the speech bubbles opposite).

> If you want to do an online activity about which countries are the richest and poorest in the world, go to www.bigpic.biz, find the playground and click on the basketball court!

> To find out more about developing countries and their debt, go to www.bigpic.biz and try an online activity, e.g. go to the classroom and click on the world map.

Activity 2 Causes of world poverty

a) Look at the opinions A–F on the right and decide whether or not you think they are convincing arguments, i.e. do you believe them?

b) Draw a line across the middle of your page and label one end 'convincing' and the other end 'not convincing'. In pairs, decide where on the line you would position each view, then write in the letters above the line.

c) Now read some of the facts below (or use the websites listed) to find out more about world poverty.

> A few hundred millionaires now own as much wealth as the world's poorest 2.5 billion people combined.

> For every $1 developing countries get from grants and aid, they owe $13 in debt to wealthier countries.

> 60 per cent of the world's poorest countries have civil conflict or war.

> 20 per cent of people living in the wealthier countries consume 86 per cent of all the goods produced in the world.

> It would take less than 1 per cent of the money spent on weapons to send every child in the developing countries to school.

Go to these websites for more information:
- www.globalissues.org
- www.oxfam.org.uk/coolplanet/index.htm
- cyberschoolbus.un.org

d) Look back at how you arranged the views given for why poverty exists in the world. Now that you have carried out research on the issue, would you make any changes? Discuss this in pairs. If you would make any changes to your answers to part **b)** then record your new answers *below* the line.

e) Share your ideas with the rest of the class and agree on the three main reasons why poverty exists in developing countries.

A
Poverty is the fault of the governments in the poor countries – their leaders are only interested in looking after themselves.

B
Those countries are poor because of all the wars and conflict that happen in them.

C
Developing countries have to deal with natural disasters like floods and droughts – that's what makes them poor.

D
It's because people in the better off countries don't care – they take advantage of the poorer countries.

E
People are poor in developing countries because of over-population – there are far too many people living in those places.

F
They have poor health care and very little education in developing countries – that's the real problem.

Activity 3 Personal journal

Draw a speech bubble in your journal and write down your own view on why poverty exists. Give reasons for your view using the facts you have gathered during your research.

24 | WHAT ARE GOVERNMENTS DOING ABOUT GLOBAL POVERTY?

Learning intentions

I am learning:
- ✓ about the goals set by the United Nations to tackle poverty
- ✓ to research and present ideas to the rest of my class.

In the last topic you learned about the causes and consequences of global poverty. In this topic you will learn about some of the ways in which we can try to make the world more equal and ensure that everyone has access to basic needs regardless of where they live.

In September 2000 the United Nations held a Millennium Summit at which the world's leaders made a promise to combat poverty across the world. They agreed a set of eight goals that they would work together to achieve by 2015. These are called the Millennium Development Goals.

Activity 1 On target?

In this activity you will find out more about the promises made by the world leaders and whether or not the world is on course to achieve these goals. By the end of the activity you should have enough information to put together a five-minute presentation on how well global poverty is being tackled.

a) Look at the opposite page: the eight Millennium Development Goals and the specific targets set by the world's leaders. Match each goal to its specific target by copying and completing the table below (the first has been done for you).

Millennium Development Goal	Target to reach by 2015
A Provide a safe and sustainable environment	3 Reduce by half the number of people who don't have a regular supply of safe water

b) Now that you have some information on the targets you can find out how well the world is doing in reaching the goals set. In groups choose one of the goals and use the following websites to investigate how much progress is being made:

- cyberschoolbus.un.org – contains facts and figures and useful video clips etc.
- www.un.org/millenniumgoals/index.html – you can use this website to find out if there are any improvements in particular countries

c) Use the information to put together a PowerPoint presentation for the rest of the class on your chosen goal. Your presentation must be able to run on its own without anyone from your group saying anything.

As a class:
d) Discuss and agree five things that make a really good presentation, e.g. images, words that people can read and understand, background music perhaps.
e) Set up your presentation for the rest of the class and watch your classmates' presentations. Use the ideas you came up with for part d) to discuss the good points of each others' presentations and to suggest improvements.

Goals

A Provide a safe and sustainable environment

B Primary education for all

C Equality for women

D Reduce the number of children dying

E Improve health of mothers

F Combat HIV/AIDS, malaria and other diseases

G Get rid of extreme poverty and hunger

H Develop a global partnership to help developing countries

Activity 2
Personal journal

Take some time to reflect on what you have seen and heard in this topic. Draw a target like the ones below and write in some facts, figures, comments that really 'hit you'. Explain underneath the target why you chose these particular points.

Targets

1 Make sure girls are not discriminated against by not getting the same education as boys

2 Half and reverse the spread of HIV/AIDS

3 Reduce by half the number of people who don't have a regular supply of safe water

4 Make sure all boys and girls get a full course of primary school education

5 Provide debt relief for the poorest countries

6 Reduce the number of children dying before the age of 5 by two-thirds

7 Reduce by 75 per cent the number of women dying during childbirth

8 Reduce by half the number of people living on a dollar a day

25 WHAT CAN I DO ABOUT GLOBAL POVERTY?

Learning intentions

I am learning:
- to evaluate the ways in which I could make a difference to the lives of people in developing countries
- how my actions and personal choices can have an effect in the rest of the world.

In the last topic you learned about what some governments are trying to do about global poverty. In this topic you will learn about some of the ways in which you as individuals and as members of society can try to make a difference to the lives of others in developing countries.

There are many organisations that are trying to tackle the issue of global poverty. Some organisations campaign against the causes of poverty, for example lobbying richer countries to 'drop the debt' of developing countries. Other organisations focus on the consequences of poverty by encouraging others to give aid and support to developing countries. There are many different ways in which you could try to make a difference to the lives of people in developing countries.

 Activity 1 Who, me? What can I do?

Try one of the online activities on the Big Pic website, www.bigpic.biz. Click on the dominoes in the bedroom, the blazer, the cash register or the water jug in the canteen.

In groups:

a) Discuss each action and rank them from the most effective to the least effective. Copy the diagram shown and write your ordering on the right-hand side of the line. (You could also add some of your own ideas.)

Action 1: Sign a petition asking the richest countries to take more action	Action 2: Attend a public rally protesting about global poverty
Action 3: Put on an assembly in school to raise awareness about global poverty	Action 4: Give money to a charity or development agency like Trocaire or Oxfam
Action 5: Have a car boot sale to raise money for a particular issue, like buying books for a school in Rwanda	Action 6: Work for a development agency when you are older
Action 7: Buy fair trade products	Action 8: Write to politicians asking them to make a difference

b) Now cross out the bottom three actions, since you consider them to be the least effective.
c) Discuss how you would re-rank the remaining actions from the most practical to the least practical and record these on the left-hand side of the line.
d) Share your top actions with the rest of the class and explain why you think this would be the best way you could contribute to tackling global poverty.

Practical | **Most** | Effective

Least

Local and Global Citizenship

There are many organisations campaigning against global poverty. They are particularly keen that young people like you get involved in their work.

Activity 2 Getting involved

In groups:

a) Choose one of the organisations below and find out about the work they do and how young people can get involved. You could visit their website or write to them for more information.

Save the Children
www.savethechildren.org.uk

Trocaire www.trocaire.org

Oxfam www.oxfam.org.uk

Make Poverty History
www.makepovertyhistory.org

Christian Aid
www.christian-aid.org.uk

Habitat for Humanity
www.habitatforhumanity.org.uk

ActionAid www.actionaid.org.uk

CAFOD www.cafod.org.uk

WaterAid www.wateraid.org

Concern www.concern.net

Activity 3 Personal journal

As well as getting involved in campaigns, we can think carefully about the personal choices we make and the impact these have on the rest of the world. Try some of the online activities suggested on the post-it on page 52. Then ask yourself if you can make even one promise to change how you 'shop'. If you can, record that promise in your journal.

b) Present your findings to the rest of the class, using a poster. Make sure your poster clearly explains what the organisation does and how young people could get involved in their work.
c) When you have looked at all the other groups' posters, put the information together in a table like this:

Organisation	What do they do?	How can young people get involved?

26 IS POVERTY A HUMAN RIGHTS ISSUE?

Learning intentions
I am learning:
- about the promises made by governments to provide people with a decent standard of living
- to organise an assembly about poverty and human rights.

In Topic 22 you discovered that social justice was about making sure that everyone had equal access to their basic needs. In Book 1 you learned that basic needs are called 'human rights'. In this topic you will find out more about the connections between social justice and human rights.

Nelson Mandela, a former President of South Africa, once said: 'Overcoming poverty is not a gesture of charity. It is an act of justice. It is the protection of a fundamental human right, the right to dignity and a decent life.'

Nelson Mandela

Most governments of the world have signed the Universal Declaration of Human Rights (UDHR) and the United Nations Convention on the Rights of the Child (UNCRC). As you know from Book 1, these are special documents which list the rights people should have because they are human beings. By signing these documents, governments have made specific promises to provide their citizens, including children, with a decent standard of living. Each promise is called an article. Some of these articles are listed below.

Activity 1
Charity or justice?

a) Rewrite the Nelson Mandela quotation in your own words. You can use the definitions below to help you.

b) Share your rewritten quote with a partner and discuss the following questions:

- What do you think is the difference between charity and justice?
- In Topic 25 you looked at how individuals could make a difference. Do you think governments could be doing more? If so, what?

justice Treating people in a morally right and fair way

charity Voluntarily giving money or help to those who need

UDHR
Article 22 You have the right to a home, enough money to live on and medical help if you are ill
Article 23 Every adult has the right to a job and to a fair wage
Article 24 You have the right to enjoy a good life. Mothers, children, the elderly and people with disabilities have the right to be cared for
Article 26 Everyone has the right to a free primary education

UNCRC
Article 19 Every child has the right to be protected from violence and abuse
Article 24 Every child has the right to the highest possible standard of health care
Article 27 Every child has the right to a decent standard of living
Article 28 Every child has the right to education and to free primary education

The four people shown here do not have access to all the rights listed, and do not have a decent standard of living.

Lydia: *I am 14 years old and I have never been to school.*

Robert: *I am 10 years old and I have no home or shelter.*

Paolo: *I am 21 years old and I cannot find a job. If I do not work I cannot get money to support my family.*

Grace: *I am 4 years old. I have malaria and there is no medicine in my village.*

Activity 2 — A right to a decent standard of living

a) Read the articles from the UDHR and UNCRC on page 54 and the statements in the speech bubbles above.

In pairs:

b) Decide which human rights, or promises made by governments, match which person. You can use the same article more than once, or even just part of the article.

c) Now copy and complete the table below to record your decisions.

Name	Basic right denied	Relevant 'promises made'
	Education	
	Health care	
	Work	
	Shelter	

d) Write a letter to your local MP explaining what you have learned in this topic. Ask them how they think the government could keep the promises they have made.

Activity 3 — Personal journal

Look at the commemorative stone and inscription. In your journal, design your own commemoration for those who have died because of extreme poverty. Use words from the UDHR or the UNCRC to help you write your own inscription.

On 17 October 1987 this commemorative stone to honour the victims of extreme poverty was laid on the Liberty and Human Rights Plaza in Paris. Similar stones have since been laid around the world. In 1992, 17 October became officially recognised as the United Nations International Day for the Eradication of Poverty. The inscription below the illustration reads:

'Wherever human beings are condemned to live in extreme poverty, human rights are violated. To come together to ensure these rights be repected is our solemn duty.' Joseph Wresinski

27 IS THERE POVERTY IN NORTHERN IRELAND?

Learning intentions

I am learning:
- to explain what is meant by the term 'relative poverty'
- about how some people in Northern Ireland have a lower standard of living than others.

On the surface in Northern Ireland we have a free education system, good housing, access to medical care and a range of jobs that people can aim to do after they leave school. But does that mean there is no poverty in Northern Ireland? The problem with poverty on a global scale is that there is inequality between those in developing countries and those in developed countries like ours. However, even within developed 'well off' countries there can still be a divide between those who have a lot and those who have, compared to the wealthy, relatively little. This is called 'relative poverty'.

Relative poverty is a real problem in Northern Ireland. The activity below will help you to identify some of the groups of people who are most affected by poverty and some of the ways in which this affects their standard of living.

Activity 1 Tackling local poverty

a) Imagine you are a local MLA (Member of the Legislative Assembly for Northern Ireland) and that the following people have come to you to ask for your support. Read what they have to say.

> Hi, my name is Sean and I work for a children's charity. Approximately 37 per cent of children under 17 live in poverty, and about 32,000 children live in 'severe poverty'. Something has to be done about this.

> Hello, I'm Jackie and I work for an organisation that supports older people. Did you know that over 17 per cent of pensioners are living in poverty? Some have to survive on just over £50 a week even though it would take about £100 a week to keep them out of poverty. What can you do to help?

> Hi, I'm Suzanne and I work for a charity that helps people who are homeless. Homelessness is a real problem in Northern Ireland. Well over 20,000 families are on waiting lists for housing and over 2500 young people are homeless. You need to do something about the situation soon.

> Hello, I'm David and I work for an anti-poverty organisation. There's still a problem with education in Northern Ireland, and a lack of education keeps people trapped in poverty. Currently 5 per cent of young people leave school with absolutely no qualifications. Nearly 25 per cent of adults have problems reading.

b) Now imagine you have organised a meeting between these people, yourself and the Minister for Social Development. Write down the main point you think each person would want to make to the Minister, and at least one thing they might want to ask the Minister to do about the situation.

> The Minister for Social Development is in charge of the Department for Social Development in Northern Ireland. The Minister's job is to tackle social disadvantage in Northern Ireland. You can find out more from the website: www.dsdni.gov.uk.

Activity 2 Meet the Minister

In a group of six:

a) Bring all your ideas together and use them to write a script for a short role-play of the meeting with Minister for Social Development.
b) Allocate a role to each member of the group: Sean, Jackie, Suzanne, David, the MLA and the Minister.
c) Perform your role-play for the rest of the class.
d) Summarise the points made and ideas suggested by each of the groups in a spidergram or table.

Activity 3
Personal journal

Think about the skills you have used in this topic and answer the following questions:

- What do you think you did well?
- What do you think you could improve upon?
- What skills did other members of your group use well?

Local and Global Citizenship

28 | HOW CAN WE TACKLE POVERTY IN NORTHERN IRELAND?

Learning intentions

I am learning:
- how Non-Governmental Organisations (NGOs) challenge poverty in Northern Ireland
- to categorise ways in which NGOs try to tackle poverty in Northern Ireland.

In Topic 27 you learned about relative poverty in Northern Ireland. In this topic you will find out about how some Non-Governmental Organisations (NGOs) are trying to tackle the problem.

Simon Community

www.simoncommunity.org

The Simon Community support people who are homeless by providing them with somewhere to live and by helping them to develop the skills they need for independent living. The also run campaigns to raise awareness about homelessness in Northern Ireland and to try to reduce the problem.

Save the Children

www.savethechildren.org.uk (follow the link to the UK then Northern Ireland)

Save the Children has been working in Northern Ireland since 1950. The main focus of the organisation is to support children living in poverty or facing discrimination. They base their work on the United Nations Convention on the Rights of the Child (see also Topic 26). Their key areas of work are poverty, education, protection of children, encouraging participation of children, promoting children's rights.

Northern Ireland Anti-Poverty Network

www.niapn.org

Northern Ireland Anti-Poverty Network works with and for those experiencing poverty in Northern Ireland. They work together with individuals experiencing poverty, the voluntary and community sector and public and statutory bodies. They run campaigns, produce information, provide poverty awareness training and research poverty issues in Northern Ireland. They aim to develop a poverty-free society.

Barnardo's Registered Charity Nos. 216250 and SCO37605

Barnardo's

www.barnardos.org.uk/northernireland.htm

Barnardo's has been working in Northern Ireland for over a hundred years. They offer a wide range of support services for children, young people and their families. For example, they help children who are young carers, looking after a sick or disabled relative. They also campaign against child poverty in Northern Ireland.

Activity 1 Each One Teach One

In groups:
a) Look at the profiles of NGOs in Northern Ireland trying to tackle poverty on page 58.
b) Choose one organisation, visit their website and find out what they are doing to tackle poverty in Northern Ireland.
c) Summarise what you have learned by completing the following tasks:
- Write down at least five facts about poverty in Northern Ireland. Write each fact on a separate strip of paper as in the example.
- Write down at least three examples of how your chosen organisation tries to tackle the issue of poverty in Northern Ireland. Write each on a separate strip as in the second example.

d) Gather the strips of paper from the whole class into a box or bag. Then each person takes out one strip and reads it carefully. It is now your job to try to teach this information to as many people as possible in the class. Move around the room passing on your information to your classmates.
e) When everyone has passed on their information to at least five other people, return to your seat and note down the following:
- as many facts about poverty in Northern Ireland as you can remember
- at least one specific example of an activity each of the NGOs is involved in.

As a class:
f) Try to group all the different activities of the NGOs together under different headings. For example:
- Which activities are mainly focused on providing services or support?
- Which are focused on helping disadvantaged people gain skills to help themselves?
- Which are focused on lobbying government, i.e. putting pressure on government to make a difference?
- Which activities are focused on raising awareness about poverty in Northern Ireland?

g) Discuss which type of activity you think would make the biggest difference to dealing with the issue of poverty in Northern Ireland.
h) Write an article for your school magazine summarising what you have learned about tackling poverty in Northern Ireland.

Did you know that children from the Travelling community are three times less likely than settled children to attend a pre-school?

Save the Children has been involved with a project called Toybox, which aims to help young Traveller children develop skills through play in their homes.

29 WHAT HAVE I LEARNED ABOUT CITIZENSHIP?

Learning intentions

I am learning:
- ✓ to use my creativity to challenge other people about social justice issues
- ✓ to reflect on the knowledge I have gained and the skills I have developed during the last set of topics.

As you know, Local and Global Citizenship is based on four themes. In this book you have explored some aspects of 'equality and social justice' and 'human rights and social responsibility'. The last few topics, in particular, have helped you understand some of the inequalities that exist in the world at both a local and global level. The next activity will give you the chance to use your creativity to show what you have learned.

Activity 1 What's the point?

a) The cartoons about development are all making a point about inequality in a global context. Look at each one carefully and write down the point you think it is trying to make.

A Source: Ammer, CWS

C Source: Schrank, CWS

B Source: Yayo, CWS

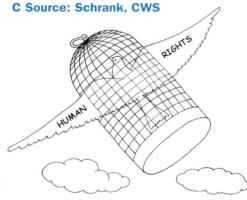

D Source: Medi, CWS

b) Which cartoon do you think has the most impact (i.e. which one makes you really stop and think about global inequalities)? Why?

c) In groups, create a cartoon to highlight what you have learned about inequalities in your local context (i.e. inequality in Northern Ireland).

d) Display your cartoons for the rest of the class and discuss what you think each one is trying to say. Which of your classmates' cartoons are the most powerful? Why?

Activity 2 Being a local and global citizen

a) Make an A3 copy of the 'Ireland in the world' diagram.

b) Think about some actions you could take to challenge inequality that would also help you develop as a socially responsible local and global citizen.

c) Record these actions on the appropriate place on the diagram, i.e. actions you could take locally in the Northern Ireland circle; actions you could take globally in the whole world circle.

	Knowing	Feeling	Doing
Before exploring these topics …	I didn't really know what discrimination was	I didn't really feel that upset about global poverty	I never would get involved in assemblies
Now …	I know how different groups of people can be affected by the treatment of others	I feel quite cross at how developing countries are treated	I want to let people know about some of the inequalities we've learned about
I would like to …	Find out more about how the government tries to tackle this	I feel I could make a difference by the actions I take here	Get involved in some action to try to change the world and make it more equal

Activity 3 Personal journal

What you learn in Local and Global Citizenship can be summed up in terms of what you know, how you feel, and what you would like to do about the issues you have been exploring. The grid gives you an example of how someone might reflect on their learning over the last set of topics. Copy the outline of the table and complete your own reflection.

30 HOW HAVE I CHANGED?

Learning intentions

I am learning:
- to identify new qualities and skills I have developed
- to set goals for Year 9.

Megan's year

During Year 8 you looked at qualities and skills for employability, deciding what they were and identifying the ones you had.

Remember, identifying and developing the skills and qualities you have will help you to decide on a job you would enjoy and do well. Employers think the qualities and skills you have are very important.

 Activity 1 Review of the year

In groups:

a) List the last 12 months. Brainstorm some of the major events and activities in your school or class last year, writing them beside the relevant month.

b) Now add any interesting things that happened to people in your group, both inside and outside school.

c) Each person in your group should now share:

- the funniest thing …
- the bravest thing …
- the most embarrassing thing …

… that happened to them last year.

d) Share your best stories with the rest of the class.

As a class:

e) Discuss how you think the last year has changed you.

As you discussed in Activity 1, last year brought many changes for you. Many of you started new schools, made new friends, studied new subjects, took part in activities you hadn't tried before. You may have travelled on a bus to school for the first time or walked home on your own, taken part in assembly or helped at a school event.

Through all of these experiences you have been developing many new qualities and skills.

Megan is a Year 9 pupil. Her teacher has asked her to think about all she has done in the last year and record this in a table.

 **Activity 2** What a difference a year makes!

a) Look at the drawings of some of the things Megan has done during the last year on page 62. Copy and complete Megan's table, matching her activities to the qualities and skills she developed. Some examples of qualities and skills are provided in the word bank below – although you may think of others.

ACTIVITY	SKILLS – I can	QUALITIES – I am
A Getting bus to and from school	• keep to set times • organise myself	• confident • independent

Word bank

Skills

work in a team   follow instructions   use the internet

word-process   work safely   give directions   organise myself

listen carefully   keep to set times   manage my time

Qualities

enthusiastic   friendly   polite   neat and tidy   encouraging

determined   responsible   confident   brave   independent

b) Think about all the things you did last year (use your work from Activity 1 to help you) and record your activities, skills and qualities in your own table. Try to identify as many new skills and qualities as possible.

Now you have reviewed your progress over the last year, you should set yourself a goal for this year. Perhaps there is a skill or quality you want to develop or improve. Maybe you want to improve in a subject in school, get on a sports team or achieve something else outside school. Remember, be realistic, not too many of us end up playing in the Premiership or winning Pop Idol!

 **Activity 3** Next, please

Identify what you want to do this year. This is your goal.

a) Write your goal at the top of your page.
b) List underneath the steps you will take to reach this goal – these are your targets.
c) Beside each target describe exactly how you will do this – these are your actions.

REVIEW I am – *below average in mathematics and disappointed.*

GOAL I want – *to finish above class average in the June mathematics exam.*

TARGETS	ACTIONS
1. Obtain a better exam mark	Attempt every question on exam paper
2. Come in top half in class tests	Spend more time revising
3. Keep notes up to date	Copy up work missed or unfinished
4. Do not fall behind in class	
5. Be organised for class	
6. Work faster	

 **Activity 4** Personal journal

How do you feel you have developed as a person after one year at high school?

Are you proud of what you achieved?

31. WHAT ARE ENTERPRISING PEOPLE LIKE?

Learning intentions

I am learning:
- ✓ examples of enterprising people
- ✓ to identify characteristics of enterprising people.

Many of you will have heard the word 'enterprise', perhaps to describe a business, a community project or even a person, but what exactly does it mean? In Topics 31–33 we will look at enterprising people to discover what they are like, think about opportunities for you to be enterprising, and find out why enterprising people make good employees.

Jim Rohn is an American motivational speaker and business leader. Here is what he says about enterprising people:

'Enterprising people are probably always on the go, never letting anything get in the way. When faced with a problem they say "Let's figure out a way to make it work" instead of "It won't work".'

'Everyone has the same 24 hours a day. Enterprising people simply do more with their 24 hours – working not harder but smarter.'

'An enterprising person is one who sees opportunity in all areas of life.'

(Source: Jim Rohn at www.nightingale.com)

Meet two enterprising people

Meet Jane

Jane Tomlinson from Leeds was diagnosed with breast cancer when she was just 26 years old.

In August 2000 a scan revealed Jane's cancer was incurable and doctors expected her to survive for only six months.

But despite the odds, Jane was determined to prove to others who are touched by cancer that life goes on and anything is possible.

Amongst her many sporting achievements, Jane is the only person with incurable cancer to complete a full Ironman (4 km swim, 180 km bike ride and 26 mile run – to be done inside 17 hours). She completed the London Marathon three times and the New York Marathon once.

Jane received many awards including the MBE in 2003. She was twice recognised at the Sportswoman of the Year Awards and was voted Most Inspirational Woman in Britain in 2003.

Sadly Jane passed away in September 2007. She raised over £1.5m for the Jane Tomlinson Appeal, which helps various charities including Macmillan Cancer Relief. (Information taken from www.janesappeal.com)

Education for Employability

Meet Adetotun

Adetotun Tomiwa is a poor young widow from a small village just outside Lagos. Until two years ago she worked side by side with her husband to make a living from the sale of wooden planks. Though things started off well, they were swindled by their suppliers and their business soon faltered.

Desperate, they applied for a small loan under the Special Programme in 2003. They bought one boar and two sows. The pigs multiplied and were sold for a good profit. Then, just over a year ago, Adetotun's husband died and she was left to pay back the loan and look after two small children alone.

She put all her energy into the pig-raising business and keeping her family alive. Today the results have paid off: she has 37 well-fed pigs and a good number are ready to be sold. She has nearly repaid the original loan and even has the money to pay an assistant to help her.

(Source: www.fao.org/newsroom)

 ## Activity 1 E is for enthusiastic!

In groups:
a) Read about Jane and Adetotun.

- Using a separate sheet for each woman, brainstorm all the skills and qualities you think each one has.
- Compare your list with the other groups in your class.
- As a class, agree on a list of qualities and skills to describe an enterprising person.

b) Using the list of skills and qualities you have come up with, try to think of a suitable word for each letter of ENTERPRISE to make an acrostic display in the classroom.

In the next topic you will look at ways *you* can be enterprising in Year 9.

 ## Activity 2
Be enterprising about enterprise!

a) Using your work from Activity 1 and the quotes from Jim Rohn, try to come up with a group definition of 'Enterprise'. Make it to the point and 'catchy'.

b) Present your definition to the class in an enterprising way, e.g. as a jingle, a rap, a poster, etc …

32 HOW CAN I BE ENTERPRISING?

Learning intentions

I am learning:
- to identify opportunities to be enterprising
- to recognise the steps involved in planning an enterprising activity
- to work as part of a team to plan an enterprising activity.

In the previous topic you learned that enterprising people are those who make things happen and get things done.

You can be enterprising in many ways, for example on the sports field, in a school play or by raising money.

In this topic you will look at examples of how other pupils have been enterprising, and together as a class plan your own enterprising activity.

 Activity 1 Good ideas

In pairs:
Look at the pupils in the pictures below and discuss how you think they are being enterprising.

Being enterprising doesn't always have to be a grand event. It can be something very simple and easy. However, it always requires planning.

Here is how one Year 9 group decided to be enterprising.

'We decided as a class to hold a disco for P7 pupils from the local primary school in our assembly hall. We made a small charge for entry and raised £80 for charity. The P7s got the chance to spend some time in the high school before they started next year, and they had a great time – as did we!'

 ## Activity 2 Perfect planning

In groups:
Make a flowchart to show all the things this group of Year 9 pupils would need to have done to organise their disco. The first few steps are done for you.

```
┌─────────────────────────────────────────┐
│      Hold the disco for P7 pupils       │
└─────────────────────────────────────────┘
                    ▲
┌─────────────────────────────────────────┐
│                                         │
└─────────────────────────────────────────┘
                    ▲
┌─────────────────────────────────────────┐
│                                         │
└─────────────────────────────────────────┘
                    ▲
┌─────────────────────────────────────────┐
│                                         │
└─────────────────────────────────────────┘
                    ▲
┌─────────────────────────────────────────┐
│     Agree on a suitable place and date  │
└─────────────────────────────────────────┘
                    ▲
┌─────────────────────────────────────────┐
│  Get permission from both school principals │
└─────────────────────────────────────────┘
```

 ## Activity 3 Our turn

a) In groups:
- Brainstorm some ideas for enterprise within your school – a project your class could do together.
- Discuss how to carry out your plan, then choose one person to present to the rest of your class.
- Once each group has presented their idea, discuss the advantages and disadvantages of each.
- Have a class vote on the one you think is best.

As a class:
b) Draw up a flowchart plan like the one in Activity 2 and put it into action.

What does an ant do when it comes across an obstacle in its path? It doesn't turn back, it climbs over, it climbs under, it goes around, no matter what effort it takes; the ant never quits looking for a way to get where it's supposed to go – ants are enterprising!

 ## Activity 4 Personal journal

There are many opportunities to be enterprising in school but think about opportunities for you to be enterprising on your own, perhaps in your home. Is there anything you could do which might improve your life or someone else's? Wouldn't it be incredible to make a difference for someone else?

33 WHY DO EMPLOYERS WANT ENTERPRISING STAFF?

Learning intentions

I am learning:
- ✓ to understand why employers want their employees to be enterprising
- ✓ to think of enterprising solutions to different work-based problems.

All employers want their employees to be enterprising! An enterprising employee is one who finds ways to improve things in the workplace. They will do things without having to be told. They can save their employer money and time, and may even come up with good ideas to improve the business they work in. Extra projects are often given to employees who demonstrate these skills.

 Activity 1 Design a supermarket

In groups:

a) Imagine a new supermarket is being built in your home town. You have been asked to design the layout of where products should be displayed.

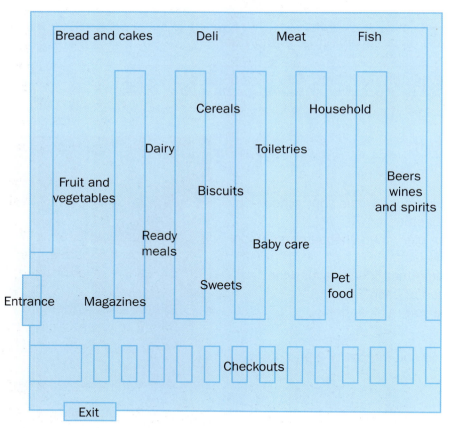

- Copy the floor plan of the supermarket onto a large piece of paper.
- List all the types of products which need to be displayed, e.g. fruit and vegetables, dairy, soft drinks etc. and find sample pictures of each in magazines.
- Discuss where to put each of your product types on your floor plan and why.
- Show where each product type should go on your floor plan by pasting on your illustrations.
- Present your plan to the rest of the class and explain the reasons for your layout.

b) At the end of this activity, discuss as a class why items are located where they are in supermarkets. For example, why do you think chocolate is placed near checkouts?

Identify how your group showed enterprise during this task. For example, how would your ideas help the supermarket to do more business?

Activity 2
Workplace enterprise

Look at the pictures of work situations today compared with those some years ago.

How has technology changed work practices, and what are the benefits to society?

Activity 3 Problems – Enterprising solutions

An enterprising employee is one who can look at a tricky situation and predict what problem might develop from it. As a result of this vision the employee can make an effort to defuse the situation before it becomes a major problem.

The following scenarios suggest a range of problems that might develop. Using your enterprise skills, how would you as a member of staff defuse or eliminate each situation? Write down the answers in your journal and discuss as a class.

Activity 4
Enterprising initiative test for new employees

You have been asked to get a large envelope containing important sets of figures to a customer 10 miles away from your place of work. They need it urgently, as a big contract they are tendering for depends upon it. If you get it to them quickly, your firm will benefit greatly from that customer's business.

a) Choose the best method of transport to get the envelope to the customer, by estimating the time and cost of each method.

b) Can you think of another method of transporting the information to the customer not referred to?

c) Decide as a class the method you would choose by discussing your reasoning.

Education for Employability

69

34 WHAT IS AN ENTREPRENEUR?

Learning intentions

I am learning:
- to define what an entrepreneur is
- to understand the difference between being enterprising and being an entrepreneur.

In Topics 31–3 you looked at being enterprising. In this topic we now consider what it means to be an entrepreneur.

Duncan Bannatyne and Deborah Meaden are both well-known, successful entrepreneurs and business people, but have more recently become famous because of the television programme *Dragons' Den*, which is all about hopeful entrepreneurs asking for help. Here are Deborah and Duncan's stories.

Duncan Bannatyne

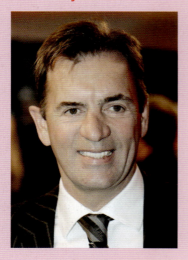

Duncan Bannatyne was not born into a wealthy family; in fact he had none of the luxuries he has now. Duncan is now thought to worth more than £170 million, so how did he do it?

He started by trading cars and then displayed his entrepreneurial skills when he purchased ice cream vans, turning them into a successful business. Always showing a willingness and enthusiasm to move on and try new things, Duncan later opened up nursing homes and more recently health clubs, hotels, casinos and bars. He holds an OBE and was recently awarded an honorary Doctor of Science (DSc) from Glasgow Caledonian University for services to business and charity.

Deborah Meaden

Deborah Meaden left school after taking her O-levels (GCSEs) and went to business college. She then started as a salesroom model in a fashion house; a few months later she moved to Italy and set up a glass and ceramics export agency, persuading shops such as Harvey Nichols to stock her products.

Then, after a stint setting up a franchise in the fashion business, she ran a prize bingo business at Butlins. 'It was fantastic. If you ask me where I learned most of my business knowledge it was there.' With three businesses under her belt she went to work with her parents in their West Star Holiday park business. She started at the bottom, but eventually led a management buy-out, doubling the profits and selling the business in a deal worth £33 million. Deborah says that her parents worked hard and she always has too. She says, 'Get on and do it, because nobody else is going to do it for you.' She now spends much of her time and money investing in new businesses.
(Source: www.guardian.co.uk)

Activity 1 Spot the difference

In groups:
a) Read Duncan and Deborah's stories on page 70, and use them as examples to discuss what you think the difference is between someone who is enterprising and an entrepreneur.
b) Make up a sentence to describe what an entrepreneur is. Share it with the rest of your class, then agree on a class definition for an entrepreneur.

In Activity 1 your conclusion may have been that you can be enterprising in lots of different situations and workplaces, but an entrepreneur will go a step further and start their own business. Here is an example of perhaps our most famous businessman, who is both enterprising but also an entrepreneur.

Richard Branson – famous multimillionaire and owner of Virgin, which comprises over 200 companies.

Richard is enterprising because while he was still at school, aged 17, he set up a student magazine, followed a year later by a student advisory service. He has made several world record attempts, both in boats and hot air balloons.

He is adventurous, energetic, tries new things and inspires others.

Richard is an entrepreneur because at the age of 20 he started his own mail order record company under the name Virgin. Two years later he owned a record studio and recorded artists including the Rolling Stones, Janet Jackson and Genesis. (Ask your parents or grandparents!!) He now has businesses in 30 countries including air travel, rail, hotels and leisure, mobile and retail businesses.

He is hard-working, forward-thinking, has vision, is a leader, is determined and takes risks.

 ## Activity 2
A little extra

In groups:
a) Using examples from the entrepreneurs featured here, identify five qualities and five skills of an entrepreneur.
b) Share these lists with the rest of the class to make a combined list; then discuss and agree on the top three qualities or skills that are needed to be an entrepreneur rather than just enterprising.
c) If possible watch an episode of *Dragons' Den*. There are some clips at www.bbc.co.uk/dragonsden. Discuss the mistakes that unsuccessful, would-be entrepreneurs make: what qualities and skills do they lack?

Education for Employability

35 COULD I BE AN ENTREPRENEUR?

Learning intentions

I am learning:
- ✓ to research entrepreneurs on the internet and present the information found
- ✓ to identify the skills and qualities of an entrepreneur
- ✓ to consider entrepreneurship as an option for me.

There are many more entrepreneurs who are very successful but never become famous. There will be entrepreneurs in the area where you live; maybe someone in your family is an entrepreneur. You could choose to tell the class about them in the next activity.

 ## Activity 1 Entrepreneur hunt

In groups:

a) Find out as much as you can about an entrepreneur. You could choose someone famous or a local entrepreneur. Here are some useful websites you could use in your research:
- www.topbusinessentrepreneurs.com
- www.entrepreneursabout.com/od/famousentrepreneurs
- www.financial-inspiration.com/famous-entrepreneurs

b) Prepare a presentation about your chosen entrepreneur to present to the rest of your class. You should include the following information:

- their background
- their business idea(s)
- how they got to where they are today
- anything else you find interesting.

Think carefully about how to present this information. You want to make it understandable, inspiring and useful. You could use ICT to create your presentation (e.g. PowerPoint, video clips, poster) or you could make an OHT or a handout.

c) How did you do? Now that you've listened and watched other presentations, how did yours compare?
Did you speak clearly, rehearse what you were going to say, use visual material like photos or video?

In your personal journal reflect on:

- what were the best class presentations and why
- what you think you did well
- what you need to improve upon next time
- what good ideas others had which would help you in your next presentation.

The need for entrepreneurs

Much employment in Northern Ireland comes from small to medium sized employers (SMEs) in businesses set up by local entrepreneurs. You will look at this in more detail in the next two topics. The economy depends on some of you leaving school

'We need to encourage creative entrepreneurial young people who can reinvigorate our economy.'
Gavin Boyd, Chief Executive Designate, Education Single Authority

and setting up your own business – you may end up being the employer for some of the other people in your class! In schools we need to encourage school leavers to consider entrepreneurship as a real option.

Entrepreneurs can be …

Potters

Ice cream vendors

Construction workers

Bakers

Hairdressers

Activity 3
Could I do it? – Personal journal

'An entrepreneur is someone who has a good idea and turns it into a successful business.'

Think or read back over the skills and qualities your class agreed were needed for an entrepreneur.

In your personal journal, copy out this definition of an entrepreneur, reflect on which of these skills and qualities you already have, and list them.

Do you think you could be an entrepreneur? Maybe you have an idea already!

If you think you couldn't be an entrepreneur, why do you feel this?

In the next topic you will meet some entrepreneurs who, like you, once sat in high schools in Ireland and wondered if they could do it – and they have!

Activity 2 Encouraging entrepreneurs

As a class:
a) Carry out a survey to see how many people would like to be an entrepreneur in your class, i.e. who would like to set up their own business?
b) Repeat the survey with an older class of pupils.
c) Are there differences between the two sets of results? If so, discuss why this might be the case.

You may have discovered that as pupils get older they are less likely to want to start their own business and that, as a result, pupils need to be continuously encouraged to think about becoming entrepreneurs.

In groups:
d) Discuss ways in which schools could encourage pupils to become entrepreneurs, and agree on one idea to share with your class.
e) Make a poster to encourage school leavers to consider becoming entrepreneurs. Perhaps these could be displayed somewhere like the careers office or in the sixth form.

36 WHO ARE THE ENTREPRENEURS IN OUR LOCAL BUSINESSES?

Learning intentions
I am learning:
- to identify what makes a successful entrepreneur
- about local entrepreneurs who contribute to the Northern Ireland economy.

As mentioned in Topic 35, small to medium employers (SMEs) are an important part of the Northern Ireland economy. (An SME is defined as employing 0–250 people, according to the EU.) This topic looks at some local entrepreneurs in SMEs, and why they are successful.

Meet Christine

Christine Boyle is Managing Director of Lawell Asphalt Roofing, operating in an industry that is generally viewed as male-dominated. Christine is living proof that the image of this industry is changing, and that a cultural shift is occurring in how women are perceived working within the construction industry. After graduating with a Social Science honours degree from Queen's University, she spent almost nine years within the financial service sector. Christine's father, who had run the family asphalt business, was nearing retirement, and was looking for the best person to carry on the family business traditions. So in 1996 Christine joined as Managing Director, and the business has gone from strength to strength.

In addition to Christine's Managing Director role, she is also chair of Women in Business NI Ltd, and is striving to make key policy-makers and decision-makers sit up and take notice of the fact that women are active entrepreneurs in the Northern Irish economy.
(Source: www.businesseye.co.uk/stories)

Christine Boyle, Managing Director of Lawell Asphalt Roofing

Activity 1 Internet search

Search the internet for information on Christine Boyle. Research the following questions, and write up your findings in your journal.

a) What management skills did Christine need to be a Managing Director?
b) Did Christine find any difficulties working in a traditionally male-dominated industry?
c) What are the qualities required for her job?
d) What part of her job as Managing Director does she find enjoyable?
e) What does Women in Business offer its members?

Discuss the results of your research in a small group. Write a brief report in your journal of this group discussion.

Some people are like Christine – they are born into a family business and therefore grow up knowing all the pressures and skills needed to run a business. The majority of people decide to start their own business in order to gain some independence, or they may have identified a special skill they have and wish to earn their living from it.

Meet Deborah

At the age of 17, Deborah already knew she had a love of art, but wasn't really sure what to do. She left school and began studying for her degree in Art, first at Magee College and then in Dublin. She soon found that ceramics was where her talent lay, and began to dream about opening her own pottery. On frequent visits home she noticed a vacant but very run-down stone building at the harbour in Dunfanaghy, which struck her as a perfect location, popular with tourists and locals. After graduating Deborah took a variety of casual jobs, but never lost sight of her dream. She began to make enquiries about how to buy the building, what planning permission would be needed to transform it, and how much that would cost. Eventually she secured a loan from the bank to purchase the old building, and then the hard work began.

Deborah Moore

After several months Muck 'n' Muffins opened its doors to the public. With a loan to pay off it was essential to bring in money quickly, so a coffee shop was located on the first floor, and an apartment on the second floor which could be rented out to visitors. The ground floor is where the kiln and wheel are located, as well as a shop for the beautiful ceramics Deborah and her sister now create. A true entrepreneur, Deborah realised that closing the doors at 5.30 p.m. was a wasted opportunity, so she now transforms the coffee shop into an atmospheric wine bar in the evenings. Deborah loves being her own boss but does work very long hours, and rarely gets to take a holiday. But she is passionate about her business, and is earning money doing something she loves.
(Source: www.mucknmuffins.com)

Muck 'n' Muffins ceramics

Activity 2   Personal journal

In the light of the work you have now done in Topics 34–36, think about whether you could be an entrepreneur by considering the following questions:

a) What really interests you?
b) Could this interest become a business idea?
c) What skills would you need to carry out your idea?

37 WHY ARE SMALL TO MEDIUM EMPLOYERS SO IMPORTANT?

Learning intentions

I am learning:
- ✓ the importance of small and medium sized businesses in my community
- ✓ how types of workplaces have changed in recent years and how this will affect the type of job I do.

Meet the residents of Stereotypical Street

 **Activity 1** The Street

Read about the people who live on Stereotypical Street.

As a class:
a) Discuss whether you think this is a typical street in your area. Why or why not?
b) Discuss what you notice about the places where most people work, and the number of people working there. Can you draw any conclusions from this?

Jim works for Samina, a firm making computer parts. There are 300 at his workplace, but Jim is being made redundant next month as his firm are opening a factory in Hungary.

Kevin works for a company which makes agricultural cooling systems. His boss started the business 15 years ago and six people now work there.

Susan came over from Lithuania two years ago. She has two jobs, one cleaning in the local high school, where there are 800 pupils and 52 staff, and then in the evenings she cleans in an estate agent's where there are six people employed during the day.

Julie works in a local florist's shop. It is owned by a girl she went to school with. There are two other women working there.

In Northern Ireland, 31 per cent of people in jobs work in the *public* sector, meaning government jobs: jobs in schools, hospitals, police, councils etc. It is expected that there will be fewer jobs in this sector in future.

All the other jobs are in what we call the *private* sector. In Northern Ireland, 90 per cent of people working in private businesses work somewhere which employs fewer than ten people.

There are now very few large employers compared with last century, because of the loss of large manufacturing businesses and changes in technology. This means there are mostly small and medium sized businesses in Northern Ireland, which we rely on to provide jobs.
(Source: DETI, March 2007)

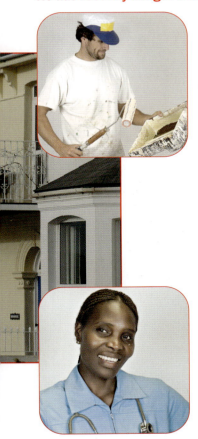

Mike is a painter and decorator. He works for himself and has a young school leaver helping him. He has recently bought a new van.

Pauline is a qualified nurse. She works at the Royal Victoria Hospital where there are some 6,000 people employed.

Activity 2 Our Street

In groups:
a) Create a poster like the previous illustration showing your own 'stereotypical street'. Each group member should contribute one person they know – finding out where they work and how many people work there.
b) Display your posters around the class, and take a tour of the village you have created as a class.
c) Does your class village reflect the current pattern of employment in Northern Ireland?

It is likely that when you start working most of your class will work in small or medium sized businesses. This may mean you have to do lots of different tasks. For example, in small hairdresser's you might be expected to answer the phone, make appointments, style hair, make coffee, tidy and clean the salon. You will need to have many skills and be adaptable. You will also be working with a small number of people for long periods of time, so you will have to learn to get on with them.

Activity 3 Personal journal

What do you think are the good and bad points of working in a small to medium sized business? What skills and qualities do you have which might help you?

Education for Employability

38 HOW DO BUSINESSES SUPPORT EACH OTHER?

Learning intentions

I am learning:
- the ways in which businesses rely on and support each other
- how my school supports local businesses.

In the previous topic we learned how many of our businesses in Northern Ireland are now small to medium sized. Many of these companies support each other by using each others' services or buying each others' goods. Smaller firms often depend on a large local employer for much of their trade. In return the smaller businesses supply them with high quality, reliable products or services. It is important that small, medium and large businesses work together to be successful and keep jobs.

RFD Beaufort Ltd in Dunmurry currently employs around 250 people. They make safety and survival equipment, such as the life jackets, life rafts and evacuation chutes you find on cruise ships and ferries. They are at the forefront of survival technology and export their goods around the world to every continent. Yet despite their international success, RFD are still supported by and give support to many local small businesses. The diagram below shows just a few examples.
(Source www.rfdbeaufort.com)

Activity 1 Working together

In groups:
a) List the different businesses RFD does business with and give examples of why and when RFD might need them.
b) Find out what type of small local businesses your school supports – do they buy in flowers for special occasions, use outside caterers, printing firms etc?

Together as a class:
c) Make a display for the wall to show how your school supports local companies.

Education for Employability

39 HOW CAN BUSINESSES MAKE THEMSELVES GREEN?

Learning intentions

I am learning:
- to be aware of 'green' issues that affect all businesses and their operations
- to focus on how we can affect global warming.

In the last topic we focused on how businesses can influence or help their local community. We are now looking at their effects on the local environment, and how individuals, communities, councils and local businesses have a definite responsibility to protect the environment.

One way in which we can all make a difference is through recycling. To help individuals and businesses, local councils have introduced recycling systems that provide us with different bins to sort our household rubbish.

Black bins are for all household waste that cannot be separated or recycled, e.g. old tea bags

Blue bins are for paper-based products, e.g. newspapers

Brown bins are for garden waste, e.g. grass cuttings

Activity 1
Waste management

In your journal, write down lists of items that should go into each of the coloured bins. Why do we now divide our household waste in this way?

Legislation from the European Union is one of the key drivers for change on waste management. They have set local councils key targets for waste disposal:

- Recovery of 40 per cent of household waste by 2010
- Diversion of 25 per cent of biodegradable municipal waste from landfills by 2010
- Diversion of 50 per cent of biodegradable municipal waste from landfills by 2013
- Diversion of 65 per cent of biodegradable municipal waste from landfills by 2020

So local councils now have to focus their thoughts on reducing waste by 65 per cent over the next decade, and landfill disposal of waste by 40 per cent. They are therefore looking at waste management as a business project which also creates employment.

This change in policy is illustrated in the Waste Management Hierarchy diagram.

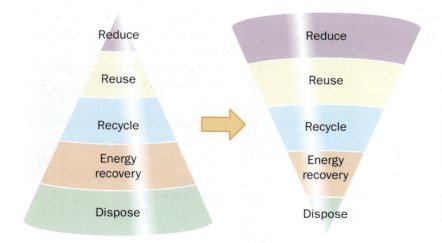

Activity 2 Guest speaker

As a class project, invite your local council's Environmental Officer into your school to give a talk on the effects that household waste is having on our planet, and how the council is creating new jobs that did not exist ten years ago to deal with waste management.

Case study: Biffa

Biffa is a leading integrated waste management business in the UK which operates across the breadth of the waste management value chain. It provides waste collection, treatment and recycling, and disposal services to around 80,000 local and national customers in the industrial, commercial and municipal sectors. (Source: www.biffa.co.uk)

Currently Biffa operate a landfill site at Hightown Road, Glengormley, Newtownabbey. The site has been designed to have a minimal effect on the landscape. Wildlife is protected within the boundaries of the quarry. Viewing platforms have been constructed to encourage the general public to view the waste management work, and how they protect the environment. This landfill site has been designed to meet EU legislation, both present and future.

Activity 3
Waste and employment

As a class, visit your local recycling plant, noting the different types of recycling skips that are available and the employment they have created. Find out how the contents of the skips are recycled and how they are reused in modern society. Present your information on your classroom noticeboard, highlighting the jobs created.

Activity 4
Waste management as a business

Read the case study on the left and look at the pictures. Search Biffa's website for any additional information. Discuss as a class the benefits of Biffa trying to protect the environment in which they operate.

Now, individually, carry out an investigation in your local area of projects that encourage the protection of the local environment. These projects may be organised by your local council, a local company or by voluntary organisations like the National Trust, Friends of the Earth etc. Present your findings to your class. Has employment been created as a result of those projects?

40 HOW DO BUSINESSES MAKE SURE THEY ARE SAFE PLACES TO WORK?

> **Learning intentions**
> *I am learning:*
> ✓ about health and safety issues in the workplace
> ✓ to raise my awareness of areas where health and safety are of importance.

Today, no matter what you do or where you are, health and safety concerns are always around you. At school there are school rules such as 'Don't run in the corridor' and 'Don't wear jewellery during PE'. As a pupil you may view rules as a form of punishment. But the reason for rules is because someone has a duty of responsibility for you. A business has a duty of care towards its customers and employees. If, by their actions, they choose to ignore the instructions they have been given, then the fault lies with the individual, not with the business.

 Activity 1 Health and safety awareness

Copy and complete the table below into your journal. List your 'school rules' and how they relate to health and safety in your school, then suggest why you think there is a need for these rules. One example has been done for you.

School rule	Possible reason for this rule
Wearing of protective goggles in science when doing particular experiments.	The wearing of goggles protects your eyes from anything that could cause damage, e.g. dangerous chemicals splashing up into your eyes.

In school you are given rules on health and safety for reasons that may not be obvious to you. In Home Economics, for example, you should always wear an overall – this not only keeps your clothes clean but also makes sure that germs do not get into the food. Look at different classrooms in school and list in your journal the health and safety notices you observe.

 Activity 2 Symbols relating to health and safety

In your journal:
a) Match the safety symbols to their descriptions.

- No mobile phones.
- A place where everyone meets during an emergency.
- Floor has just been washed.
- Exit to be used in case of an emergency.
- First Aid facilities available.
- Lights to be switched off when not in use.
- Running can be dangerous.

b) Where would you see each symbol displayed?
c) What health and safety issue does each refer to?
d) Why do you think symbols have been used rather than words?

Health and safety is a very important consideration for anyone setting up a new business, and there are many laws relating to health and safety which businesses must follow. A good example is the food industry, where the premises must be kept to a very high standard. Government health inspectors make regular visits to inspect how food is being stored, how clean kitchens are, and what facilities are available for staff to wash their hands etc.

Case study: Whose fault is it?

Joanna is 17, and works in the local bakery every Saturday and during school holidays. She carries out a number of duties, one of which is cleaning out the industrial food mixer.

The owner of the business is Joe, who is very strict about keeping everything clean and safe. When a new employee starts working in his bakery, he always spends time going over the health and safety issues.

Clare, a new 16-year-old employee, has just started work in the bakery. After supervising Clare for most of the day, Joe leaves her helping Joanna to clean the food mixer. Clare is fooling around with Joanna, throwing surplus 'dough' at her which lands in her hair. Joanna's long hair, which has been tied up, comes apart and gets caught in the food mixer while it is being cleaned. Joe comes into the work area and quickly switches off the food mixer before any real damage can be caused.

Activity 3 — Health and safety issues in the workplace

Read the case study and answer the following questions in your journal.

- Placing yourself in Joe's position, what action would you take?
- Was there any danger to anyone?
- Who was at fault? Joe? Joanna? Clare? Everyone?
- Could the situation with Joanna's hair have been avoided?
- What was the health and safety issue?
- Does age play a part in this situation?

a) Discuss in detail with your class and teacher the full implications of the case study.

b) Can you give a personal example of a health and safety issue for the class to discuss?

41. HOW CAN I LEARN TO BE A RESPONSIBLE EMPLOYEE?

Learning intentions

I am learning:
- ✓ to be responsible for my actions at home and at school
- ✓ to learn about rules within the work environment that are for my benefit.

In Topic 40 you learned that the individual has responsibility for health and safety as well as the organisation. In this topic we look at other responsibilities we have as individuals at school, at home and in the workplace.

We all have responsibilities. For example, we are responsible for the actions or deeds that we perform. If you push someone, even as a joke, and the person gets hurt you are responsible. If you fail to attend a school presentation that recognises your peer group's achievements, you are held responsible for that absence. As a school pupil you have a range of responsibilities, for example:

- Completing homework to the best of your ability
- Working as part of a team in school
- Reporting bullying

✓✗ Activity 1 My individual responsibilities

a) Copy and complete the table below to list ten responsibilities that you have at school and ten at home. Two examples have been done for you.

Responsibilities at school	Responsibilities at home
1 To attend all classes on time	1 To look after my little brother/sister
2	2

As a class:

b) Discuss these lists and come up with a class list of responsibilities you all have at school and at home.

c) In your journal list five responsibilities that could be transferred into the workplace, e.g. 'To attend all classes on time' – 'To be in work on time'.

When you start employment with a company, the company will generally give you a list of job tasks and certain duties that they expect you to carry out. This is referred to as a 'Job Description'. When you have read through the Job Description you will be asked to sign a document or indicate that you are in agreement with what is being asked of you.

Job Description

The person appointed must carry out the following duties:

- Process invoices as required
- Develop an electronic filing system to meet organisational needs
- Liaise with other internal departments
- Work to maintain good customer relationships
- Any other duties as directed

Activity 2
Job Description

As a group:
Discuss 'the responsibilities' that you would expect to go with each of the duties, e.g.:

- Work to maintain good customer relationships
- Be pleasant to all customers at all times, even when …

Activity 3 Jobs and responsibilities

Look through your local newspaper and select a job you might be interested in. Most companies now put their jobs on the internet, so you can download a Job Description and Application Form for that particular job. Or you could try the website www.LoadzaJobs.co.uk and download a sample Job Description.

In small groups:
a) Compare the Job Descriptions of the different jobs and discuss how the employee will be expected to act responsibly.

As a class:
b) Discuss how you think the employer decided to describe the employee's responsibilities.

Activity 4
Debating the subject of responsibility

Organise in your class group a debate on the issue of 'Being responsible'.

Divide your class into three groups:

1. A group to debate *for* being responsible.
2. A group to debate *against* being responsible.
3. A group to act as *judge* as to which group put the stronger case during the debate.

Discuss all the major points and record in your journal the areas where agreement was reached.

Education for Employability

42 WHY IS TEAMWORK SO IMPORTANT IN THE WORKPLACE?

Learning intentions

I am learning:
- ✓ to understand the benefits of teamwork
- ✓ why employers look for evidence of teamwork skills and qualities.

Sometimes problems are more easily solved, or work can be done more quickly and efficiently, if more people are contributing to the solution. The principal of your school cannot run the school alone, so they delegate certain jobs. In the world of work, businesses can only function as a direct result of teamwork.

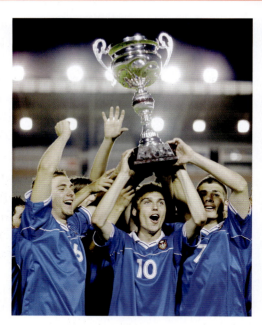

 **Activity 1**
Case study of a school department

There are three members of staff in a particular department. They all teach both junior and senior school. One member of staff teaches Y11, while another teaches Y12. All teach junior school classes, and every three years on a rotation system one member of staff will focus on teaching junior school only. The teachers are allocated a particular class in junior school to teach, but they change around so that pupils get the benefit of a change in teaching style. All three teachers encourage pupils to express themselves in a constructive manner. The three teachers are very friendly, not only with pupils but with each other. It is very clear that the teachers all rely on each other for help and support.

a) What makes this a good department, in your opinion?
b) Do you think it is a productive department, i.e. would pupils like going to that department?
c) Do you think there's laughter in the department, or is it a very serious environment?

Write in your journal your views of what makes it a good department to work in.

Some of the main pointers that a business will look for in any new employee are:

- Is that person a team player?
- Will the new employee be an asset to the business?
- Is the new employee motivated to work well on their own and with others?

Activity 2 Teamwork problem

You have been given a task to cross a river which is 15 cm deep but 5 m wide. There are five individuals within your party. You must cross the imaginary river without getting your feet or body wet. At one point in this task all five must be standing in the river. How do you as a group cross the river using any resources you can find?

Being a good team player and a hard worker is something to start working on now. Your school will help you develop these skills, through group work in class and by giving you the opportunity to take part in extra-curricular activities, such as school choir, sports teams, chess clubs and drama clubs; the rest is up to you!

As well as looking at exam results, employers will look for evidence of your teamworking skills through other activities you have taken part in. This will often have an influence on whether they interview you or offer you a job.

Activity 3 Extra-curricular teamwork skills

a) Carry out a class survey to find out what activities people in your class take part in which would give evidence to an employer of good teamwork.

As a class:
b) Discuss what personal qualities each activity would show to any employer.
c) In your journal copy and complete the table below to record your findings. Two examples have been done for you.

As a class:
d) Discuss the benefits of extra-curricular activities as a method of developing teamwork.

Activities with a school base	Personal qualities	Activities outside the school	Personal qualities
1 Art club	You have good hand and eye co-ordination	1 Competitive team cycling	You work as a team to achieve group goals
2		2	

43 WHAT TYPE OF JOB WILL I DO?

Learning intentions

I am learning:
- the different job families
- the reason why jobs are grouped together
- to match qualities and skills to job families
- to start considering the types of jobs which suit my qualities and skills.

Throughout this year and last year you have been learning about identifying your own qualities and skills. You are most likely to enjoy and succeed in a job that matches those qualities and skills.

With so many different jobs around, how do you start to choose?

At this stage you are not expected to pick the perfect job for you, but you can start to identify areas that might suit you, or areas you already know you wouldn't enjoy.

There are so many different jobs that one step is to group them together in what we sometimes call 'job families'. Each family contains jobs that require similar personal qualities and skills, and involve similar types of work. The differences may be in the qualifications required for each job, or a change in context, for example caring for elderly people rather than children.

The main job families are:

Scientific/investigative, e.g. dietician

Organisational/administrative, e.g. insurance

Artistic, e.g. hairdresser

Social, e.g. nurse

Practical, e.g. plumber

Enterprising, e.g. estate agent

Education for Employability

Activity 1 Appropriate skills

In pairs:
Read the statements below and match each with an appropriate job family.

You enjoy being creative. You have good ideas and like to work alone. You have imagination.

You like to use your hands, you enjoy building and making things, you enjoy using tools and machinery. You like to take action rather than talk about something.

You are a good leader; you can encourage others and are enthusiastic. You are a good communicator and are good at persuading people.

You are a caring person who likes helping others. You are a people person.

You enjoy a challenge and like solving problems. You like to try new things and probably enjoy science and maths.

 ## Activity 2 Happy families

As a class:
a) Each of you write one of these jobs on a post-it note.
b) Around the classroom place six large pieces of paper with one job family heading on each.
c) Stick your job onto the sheet of the family you think it belongs in.
d) Discuss as a class any you feel are in the wrong place and why.

The good thing about job families is that they can lead you on to consider a job that is linked to what you had thought of before and find it suits you even better. Career websites and packages such as Odyssey often have links to related jobs. You will look at this more next year.

 ## Activity 3
Personal journal

Read over the descriptions of the job families and think about the type of person you are. What are your feelings about these groups: are there any you think suit you more than others, or are there any you feel you definitely wouldn't like?

Write your ideas down – and good luck!

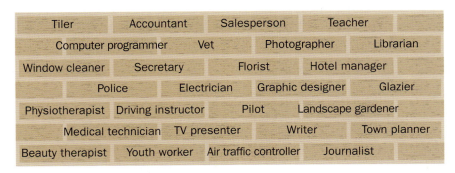

Tiler, Accountant, Salesperson, Teacher, Computer programmer, Vet, Photographer, Librarian, Window cleaner, Secretary, Florist, Hotel manager, Police, Electrician, Graphic designer, Glazier, Physiotherapist, Driving instructor, Pilot, Landscape gardener, Medical technician, TV presenter, Writer, Town planner, Beauty therapist, Youth worker, Air traffic controller, Journalist

ANSWERS

Answers to Topic 18

1. religious belief
2. political opinion
4. age
5. ethnic group
7. sexual orientation
8. gender
9. whether they have disabilities or not
12. whether they have dependants or not
14. whether they are married or not

Answers to Topic 23

1. FALSE: There are 100 million homeless people.
2. TRUE: And over 1 billion people live on less than $1 a day.
3. FALSE: 1 billion people cannot read or write.
4. FALSE: 30 per cent of people do not have access to safe water.
5. FALSE: It's actually 2 million children who die of preventable diseases.

INDEX

A
activities 1
addiction 30–1
advocacy 44
aggressive behaviour 21
assertive behaviour 20–1
assess risk 14

B
Bannatyne, Duncan 70
Barnardo's 58
basic assertiveness 20
basic needs 46–7
Biffa 81
bins for recycling 80
Boyle, Christine 74–5
Branson, Richard 71
businesses
   discrimination in 36, 37
   entrepreneurs in local 74–5
   green 80–1
   health and safety 82–3
   small to medium employers (SMEs) 72, 74, 76–7
   supporting each other 78–9
   teamwork in 86–7

C
career websites 89
changes in Year 7 and 8 62–3
charity 54
citizenship 60–1
commemorative stone 55
confidence 4–5

D
delayed gratification 10–11
developing countries
   debts 49, 52
   poverty in 48–9
discrimination 34–41
   causes of 34–5
   laws to protect against 38–9
   role of the Equality Commission 40–1
   types of 36–7
Dragons' Den 70
drugs 26–9
   meaning of the word 'drug' 26
   medical use of 26
   recreational use of 27–9

E
Edison, Thomas A. 24
emotional safety 16–17, 18
   in a difficult situation 16
empathetic assertiveness 20
employers and the skills they look for 62, 68–9, 87
employment
   enterprising staff in 68–9
   Job Descriptions 85
   private sector 77
   public sector 77
   responsible employees 84–5
   skills and qualities for 62, 68–9, 87
   teamwork in 86–7
   types of 88–9
   in waste management 80–1
enterprising people 64–9
   Adetotun Toniwa 65
   encouraging pupils to become 66–7
   Jane Tomlinson 64
   Richard Branson 71
   in the workplace 68–9
entrepreneurs 70–5
   Christine Boyle 74
   Deborah Meaden 70
   Deborah Moore 75
   Duncan Bannatyne 70
   encouraging young 72–3
   a need for 72–3
   in Northern Ireland 74–5
   Richard Branson 71
environment, protecting the 80–1
equality 32–3
   and meeting people's basic needs 46–7
   and Non-Governmental Organisations (NGOs) 44–5
   promoting 42–5
Equality Commission 40–1
equality law 38–41
escalating assertiveness 20
ethnic groups, discrimination against 36, 37
European Union 80

F
feelings
   boys and girls expressing 17
   in a difficult situation 16
   expressing negative 20
   managing 16–17
food industry 83
football, girls playing 32

G
global poverty *see* poverty
goals for Year 9 63
gratification, delayed and instant 10–11

H
health and safety 82–3
health inspectors 83
household waste 80–1
human rights 32
   and poverty 54–5

I
'I AM' risk management process 14–15
identify risk 14
imagination 12–13
impulses 10, 11
individual responsibilities 84–5
instant gratification 10–11

J
Job Descriptions 85
job families 88–9
jobs
   types of 88–9
   see also employment
justice 54
   see also social justice

L
landfill sites 81
Lawell Asphalt Roofing 74
learning from mistakes 24–5
learning intentions 1
learning to trust 18–19
legislation, equality 38–41
local councils 80–1
Loren, Sophia 24
Luther King, Martin 33

M

Magee, William Connor 24
manage risk 14
Mandela, Nelson 54
Maslow, Abraham 46
Maslow's pyramid of need 46
Meaden, Deborah 70
Merry, Philip 19
migrant workers 34, 42
Millennium Development Goals 50
Minister for Social Development 57
mistakes, learning from 24–5
Moore, Deborah 75
moral code, personal 22–3

N

needs, meeting people's 46–7
negative thoughts 6–7
Non-Governmental Organisations (NGOs)
  promoting equality 44–5
  tackling global poverty 52–3
  tackling poverty in Northern Ireland 58–9
Northern Ireland
  discrimination against migrant workers 34
  employment in 72–3, 77
  Equality Commission 40–1
  equality law 38–41
  local entrepreneurs 74–5
  Minister for Social Development 57
  need for entrepreneurs in 72–3
  poverty in 56–9
  prejudice in 34
  small to medium employers (SMEs) 72, 74, 76–7
Northern Ireland Act (1998) Section 75 38
Northern Ireland Anti-Poverty Network 58

O

optimism 6, 7
organisations see Non-Governmental Organisations (NGOs)

P

patience 10–11
personal capabilities 1
personal journal 1
personal moral code 22–3
personal responsibility 8–9, 84–5
pessimism 6, 7
positive thinking 6–7
poverty 48–59
  absolute 48
  causes of global 48–9
  commemorative stone in Paris 55
  government actions to reduce global 50–1
  and human rights 54–5
  individual actions to make a difference 52–3
  moderate 48
  Non-Governmental Organisations (NGOs) tackling 52–3, 58–9
  in Northern Ireland 56–9
  relative 56–7
prejudices 34, 35
private sector 77
progress in Year 8 62–3
public sector 77

Q

qualities
  developing new 62–3
  matching with a job 88–9
word bank 63
see also skills

R

racist crimes 36
recycling 80–1
relative poverty 56–7
responsibility, individual 8–9, 84–5
RFD Beaufort Ltd 78
RICE analysis 18–19
right or wrong, deciding on 22–3
risks
  of exposing true emotions 16–17
  'I AM' risk management process 14–15
Roberts, Wess 24
Rohn, Jim 64

S

Sagan, Carl 12
Sandburg, Carl 13
Save the Children 53, 58, 59
school rules 82
self, true 2–3
self-confidence 4–5
self-talk 6–7
Shaw, George Bernard 12
Simon Community 58
skills
  being enterprising 68–9
  and capabilities 1
  developing new 62–3
  matching with a job 88–9
  in small or medium sized businesses 77
  teamworking 87
  word bank 63
small to medium employers (SMEs) 72, 74, 76–7
  supporting each other 78–9
social justice 46–7
  and human rights 54–5
stereotypes 34, 35
success 25

T

teamwork in businesses 86–7
thinking positively 6–7
thinking skills 1
'this makes me feel' language 20
Tomiwa, Adetotun 65
Tomlinson, Jane 64
travelling community 59
true self 2–3
trust, learning to 18–19

U

United Nations Convention on the Rights of the Child (UNCRC) 54
United Nations Millennium Summit 50
Universal Declaration of Human Rights (UDHR) 32, 54

V

Virgin 71

W

waste management 80–1
Waste Management Hierarchy 80
Watson, Thomas J. 25
wheelchair users 37
will 10, 11
World Bank 48

Y

Year 7 and 8, changes in 62–3
Year 9 goals 63